The Cleggan Bay Disaster

Best wishes

M. Feeney.

A donation has been made to the
Royal National Lifeboat Institution (RNLI)
in respect of the sale of this book.

The Cleggan Bay Disaster

*An account of the savage storm
in October 1927 that devastated
the Connemara communities
of Rossadilisk and Inishbofin*

MARIE FEENEY

PENUMBRA PRESS 2001

First published 2001 in Ireland by
Penumbra Press
Largynaseeragh, Glencolumbkille, Co Donegal

Third impression 2006

ISBN 0-9541265-0-5

Design and typesetting by
Jane Stark

Production assistant
Gráinne Stark

Printed and bound in Spain by
GraphyCems, Villatuerta, Navarra

CONTENTS

DEDICATION

*Dedicated to the memory of
the fishermen who drowned
on 28th October 1927,
to their families, and all those
who lost their lives at sea,
in search of a living.*

FOREWORD

SEA AND WATER TRAGEDIES have long had a special resonance in Society. One only has to think of *Eanach Cuan* or the Sean nos song *Currachai na Tra Baine* or even the fascination with the *Titanic* to appreciate this.

The Cleggan Bay disaster was another such tragedy, which has since it happened, been part of the folklore of Connemara. Indeed Walter Macken wove the disaster and its terrible consequences into his book *Rain on the Wind.*

Sea disasters are often filled with pathos due to their unexpectedness and their manifestation of the terrible and awesome power of the elements. Looking at the sea on a calm day, it is hard to imagine the ferocity of the storm and its consequences. It was exactly this set of circumstances that led to the horrendous Cleggan Bay disaster, the effects of which are still felt in the Rossadilisk (Cleggan) district and on neighbouring Inishbofin Island.

As the 75th anniversary of the disaster approaches, it is fitting that a book has been written on the subject, while people are still alive who have an intimate knowledge of what happened.

That a young person from the area, Marie Feeney, would undertake this project is a tribute to how the memory of this terrible day is still alive in the area.

Her research, both local and national, has been thorough and mixes documentary records with local memory. While giving an accurate account of the facts, she manages to convey the scale of the human tragedy involved.

The book also records similar tragedies on the same night, off the Inniskea islands and Lacken in North Mayo, giving a feel for the common vulnerability of coastal communities eking a living from fishing in a battle against the seas.

National history is often the accumulation of local events woven in a pattern. The Cleggan Bay disaster was one of these events, which stirred the conscience of the nation and prompted Government action.

This comprehensive recording of the event and its aftermath, complete with photographs, is due to the diligence and interest of Marie Feeney in recording for posterity this terrible tragedy; best summed up in the lament by Agnes Lynam, a young widow, which concludes with the lines.

My man is gone, he is young to die
And I am left alone, mavrone.

Éamon Ó Cuív, T.D.,
Aire Stait

INTRODUCTION

THE SMALL FISHING VILLAGE OF CLEGGAN and its offshore neighbour, the island of Inishbofin, share a history that has been shaped, in large degree, by their location. Poised on the jagged western edge of Ireland, in the shadow of mountains that rise abruptly from the sea, the two communities have been honed by salt-laden winds, pounding Atlantic waves and a moist oceanic climate. Before the advent of modern roads and communication systems, the spectacular landscape of bogs, mountains and lakes formed a natural barrier between Connemara and the rest of the country. Self-reliance, resourcefulness, close knit family ties and a strong religious faith were their bulwarks against the relentless challenges of living in such a harsh environment.

This is the story of one fateful night in the life of those two communities – a night that changed the course of local history and had repercussions for decades afterwards. Although it is the story of one specific maritime tragedy in the west of Ireland, it is one that will strike familiar chords in small fishing communities, not only around the coast of Ireland, but anywhere that people pit their wits and strength against weather and ocean. It will evoke particular memories in the inhabitants of Inniskea and Lachan Bay in County Mayo, for whom the night of October 28th 1927 was also one of great horror and tragedy.

My own interest in this part of our local heritage comes from the fact that my grandfather, Festy Feeney, was one of the survivors from Rossadilisk (Cleggan). From a very early age I learned all about him and his life from Festy Lacey (RIP), another elderly man from Rossadilisk who acted as my substitute grandfather. Much has been written and told about the Cleggan Bay Disaster, and I am very grateful to all those who have helped me with my research by sharing their memories so openly with me.

Times have changed and, thanks to modern technology, improved infrastructure and efficient rescue services such as the RNLI, the number of such tragedies has considerably decreased. Fishing is no longer the mainstay of coastal communities, which now depend on new sources of income such as tourism. For many of today's generation, events like the Cleggan Bay Disaster of 1927 are wrapped in the mists of local folklore. Eyewitnesses to that terrible night are rapidly disappearing with the passage of time. I hope that in some small way this book will serve as a tribute to all those who lost their lives and to all who were left behind to carry on.

I would like to extend special thanks to all those who contributed to the publication of this book:

Michael and Marion Feeney; Bridie Mulkerrins; Minister Éamon Ó Cuív, TD; Sínead Flaherty; Maureen Davin; Amy Loughlin; Brian O'Donnell; Mary Ruddy; The Ryan (Murray) family, Westport; Noel Schofield; Mary Lavelle; Kieran Concannon, Marie Coyne; Oliver Coyne; John, Neill and David Stenston; Eddie Devane; Phyllis O'Donaghue; Agatha Burke; Cormac Ó Cionnaith; Hugh Musgrave; Deirdre Shanahan; Pamela Lacey; John Hughes AIB Clifden; Paddy FitzPatrick; Pádhraic Ó Láimhín; Frank McMullan A.F.A.I.P.; John Abeyta and Ann Prendergast.

John O'Halloran and Dr Evelyn Musgrave died before the publication of this book, but both contributed a great deal to it, and welcomed me into their homes with open hearts.

My gratitude also goes to the National Archives; *Connacht Tribune* and *Connacht Sentinel*; *Irish Independent*; *Irish Times*; *Mayo News*; Island House, Galway; National Census Board; Inishbofin Development Association Committee and all those who contributed photographs and drawings.

The author and publishers would be most grateful for any errors or omissions to be brought to their attention in order that they may be corrected in the next edition.

SETTING THE SCENE

IN THE EARLY TWENTIETH CENTURY, the people of Cleggan and Inishbofin lived simple lives on virtually valueless pieces of land that generally measured no more than two acres. The rock-strewn landscape, with its shallow soil and lack of shelter from harsh Atlantic winds, yielded a meagre existence, but the inhabitants made ends meet by sowing crops of potatoes, carrots and onions, using seaweed and manure as fertiliser. Some of the old cultivation ridges (known locally as lazy beds), where the potatoes and vegetables were sown, can still be seen today around the area. For additional nourishment and income, the people turned to the sea.

During a typical year every season brought with it plenty of work that needed to be done. Neighbours helped each other in a kind of bartering system. In the months when bad weather prevented fishing, there was still a great deal of work to do as nets were mended, boats tarred and lobster pots woven. Pots were constructed from sally (willow) rods, which were stuck into the earth in a circular pattern in order to weave them into the traditional basket shape.

Drawing by Pamela Lacey

In March it was time to cut the turf. Using a slean (a long, narrow spade specially designed for the purpose) the men cut the sods of turf from the bog and the children would spread them out to dry. Once the turf had lost some of its moisture, women and children would arrange the sods in small stacks, in a process known as 'footing'. This would further dry out the turf to a point where it could be gathered and loaded into large willow baskets and taken home by donkey.

The land was tilled during the same period, followed by the sowing of seed potatoes and the rest of the vegetables. Farmers who had enough land would save hay from their fields during the months of June and July. At the same time, fishing would continue. The women would tend the home and family, with chores such as knitting, sewing and baking being part of their daily routines all year round.

Men were usually dominant in the household, and regarded by outsiders as the representative of the whole family. All decisions about farming and fishing were made by them. Women, however, exerted considerable influence within the household through their care and direction of the children. Husbands and wives had their individual tasks to perform within the family, in most cases displaying a mutual respect for each other's role.

According to John O'Halloran of Inishbofin, people in the two communities were generally happy and content. Frequent social contact was maintained between the island and the mainland in spite of the six mile stretch of water that separated them. He recalled that he and his father used to row regularly from Inishbofin to the village of Rossadilisk to visit friends during the winter months.

They would leave the island around one o'clock on a Sunday afternoon and stay until after dark in one of the farmhouses, or sometimes they would spend the night. Some of the Rossadilisk residents had relatives on Inishbofin and as the word spread around the village that John and his father had arrived, they would eagerly gather round them to inquire about news from the island.

Up to thirty people would assemble in one small cottage to entertain one another telling stories, singing songs and playing cards. The cabin was lit by oil lamps and candles. Oil for the lamps was extracted from fish such as pollock, and burned with the aid of a piece of straw or a rush.

The women of the house baked their traditional brown bread during the day and that was eaten with homemade butter, which would have been churned by the younger members of the family using milk from their cow.

In this closely knit community many were related. Second cousins were as important as sisters and brothers in these extended families. It was not uncommon for a couple in the early part of the twentieth

CENSUS FIGURES 1911

TOTAL NUMBER OF PERSONS:
Cleggan 538
Inishbofin 801

NUMBER OF ACRES:
Cleggan 4,737
Inishbofin 3,264

CENSUS FIGURES 1926

CLEGGAN
Total number of persons: 414 (23% decrease)
Males: 205 Females: 209
Valuation of land: £832.00

INISHBOFIN
Total number of persons: 612 (23.6% decrease)
Males: 337 Females: 275
Valuation of land: £652.00

CENSUS FIGURES 1936

CLEGGAN
Total number of persons: 336 (18.8% decrease)
Males: 161 Females: 175
Valuation of land: £870.00

INISHBOFIN
Total number of persons: 510 (16.7% decrease)
Males: 296 Females: 214
Valuation of land: £652.00

century to have up to ten children. Immigration was relatively uncommon in the area during the 1920s and census figures indicate that it was not until the 1940s that the population started to decline as more people left to seek their fortune overseas.

Given the number of mouths to feed and the limited resources on land, the sea provided a much needed income for the people of Rossadilisk and Inishbofin.

Fishing in the west of Ireland
The main harvests from the sea were herring and mackerel, which gathered in large shoals off Ireland's west coast. Most of the catch was salted and exported. This trade reached its peak about 1908, when an extension was added to Cleggan Pier.

Barrels of salt were imported from Germany by rail to the nearby station at Clifden. Salting took place on the piers at Cleggan and Inishbofin, where buyers or their agents would come to purchase the fish. Thomas Nee was one such direct buyer from the area, and he used to charter a boat from the Limerick Steamship Company to take the fish to Germany and the American markets. The railway link from Clifden, which opened in 1885, also enabled the export of fresh fish for sale to the London market within twenty-four hours of leaving the area. This trade provided an important income for the local population and helped them to achieve a better standard of living.

In the two communities, all crews went out to sea at the same time and very rarely moved more than about four miles from their homes. When times were bad, the fishermen shared what little they might have caught. Each crew always fished within shouting distance of the other boats. Most of the fishermen were unable to swim, because many of them shared my grandfather's belief that if you couldn't swim, you were more likely to be careful; moreover, if you knew how to swim, it would prolong the struggle for life.

Fishermen maintained a strong Catholic tradition, and never went fishing on a Sunday unless they had first been to Mass. Under the stern of the boat they kept a bottle of holy water, and when it came time to set their nets they would do so 'In the name of the Father, the Son and the Holy Ghost, Amen'. They were of the belief that, just like the disciples of Jesus, some of whom were also fishermen, they

Photograph courtesy of Oliver Coyne, Cleggan

THE BOATS AND THEIR OWNERS

(recalled by John O'Halloran)

BOFIN NOBBIES

The Glorious	Pat Burke
The Star	James Concannon
St. Colman	Michael Murray
The Dolphin	Pat Davis
The Clara	Michael O'Halloran
The Little Monica	John Prendergast
St. Peter	Patrick Tierney

CLEGGAN NOBBIES

St. Mary	Festy Feeney
The Herman	Michael Lacey
The Gardnet	Matty de Van (Ballinakill)

Drawing by Deirdre Shanahan

were at the mercy of the sea and of God. At six o'clock in the evening, while at sea, they would cease all work, sit on the wooden seats in their boats and recite the rosary. The vessels used by the fishermen around 1905 in Rossadilisk and Bofin were called pucans. Slightly larger than the traditional currach (locally known as canoes at that time), these boats were around 22 feet long, with up to seven nets, and usually held a crew of five men. The men propelled the boats by means of wooden oars and, depending on the weather, they sometimes used a sail. Drift netting was the usual method of fishing. The nets would float in an upright position near the surface, creating a wall into which the shoals of mackerel and herring would swim.

Around 1909, as John O'Halloran recalled, the Congested Districts Board introduced a boat called the nobby to the area. These boats, similar to the Galway hooker, were about 45 feet in length and had sails. The nobbies were anchored offshore and the men would row out to them from their homes each day, using one of their currachs. These larger vessels allowed the fishermen to venture further afield, resulting in more plentiful catches of fish. The men of the two

Cleggan quay (Photograph courtesy of Oliver Coyne, Cleggan)

communities invested in more nets, with some boats having up to fifteen nets on board. This time of relative plenty, when fishermen were able to pay the loans they had taken out for fishing gear, was destined not to last. A decade later, in 1919, the nobby boats, along with their nets, were rotting away on the shorelines of Inishbofin and Rossadilisk, as poor catches drastically reduced the viability of the industry.

The villagers were once again left with very little on which to live. Some relief was experienced when the lobster fishing industry began in Cleggan on a small scale around the 1920s, with a buyer called Marcel Samzun exporting the catches to France. The fishermen were careful not to take more than their share of lobsters, guided by a tradition in those days to limit the number of pots that they used to 33 – one for each year that Christ lived on earth. What may now seem like superstition had the effect of preventing the depletion of stocks that plagues today's fishing industry.

In the summer of 1927, the mackerel and herring again danced in Cleggan Bay, and life once more took a turn for the better, but such good fortune was to be shortlived. Later in the season, events would take place that were to change their lives forever.

Left: *An example of the plentiful catches made by fishermen in the years preceding the disaster of 1927.* (Photograph courtesy of the *Irish Independent*)

Below: *A curragh on Cleggan Bay in the 1990s.* (Photograph by Marie Feeney)

Opposite: *Mikie O'Halloran, with lobster pots outside his cottage on Inishbofin.* (Photograph courtesy of Ann Prendergast)

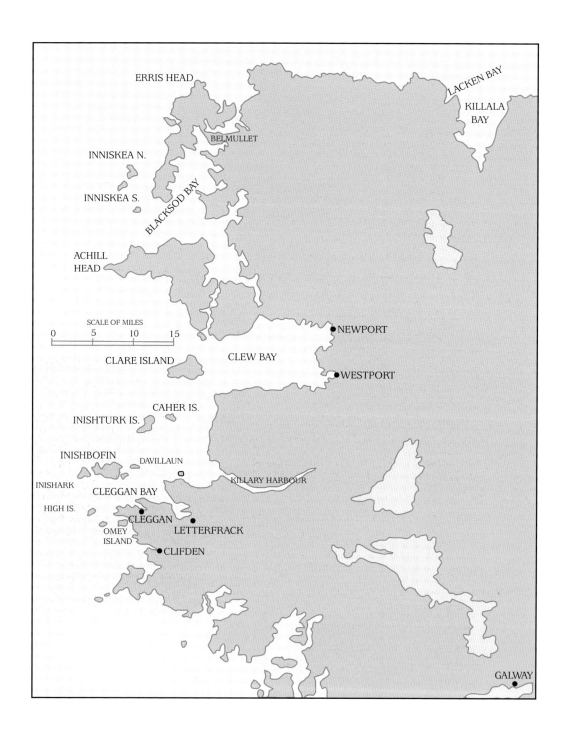

FRIDAY OCTOBER 28th 1927

On Friday evening, October 28th 1927, the weather was calm, with light rain falling in a gentle northwest wind. The sea was as smooth as a lake. It had been a busy day for the people of Cleggan, as they made preparations for a community dance (ceili), which was to be held in a shed across from Johnny Coyne's Bar in the centre of the village. Tragically, the memories associated with that venue would not be the happy ones so eagerly anticipated by the villagers.

At around five o'clock that evening, four boats pushed off from Rossadilisk and another five boats left the east end of Inishbofin. At about the same time, in neighbouring County Mayo, fishermen also set out from Lacken Bay and Inniskea.

A little over an hour later, the Rossadilisk crews started shooting their nets. A quarter of a mile away, along the shoreline of Cleggan Bay, their family cottages were still in view as a gale lunged at the group of fishing boats seemingly from nowhere, tossing the small craft skywards on the crests of mountainous waves. Moments later, as their boats plunged downwards, the force of the water cascaded around the men, sending them reeling blindly around their boats.

As the storm hit the boats out in the bay, a retired doctor was listening to the weather forecast on a magnetic radio, attached by wires to two poles outside his little cottage at Cleggan Farm. When

Dr Holberton (photograph courtesy of the late Dr Evelyn Musgrave)

Dr Holberton heard the storm warning, he immediately called his farmhand, Tommy Mullen, and urged him to go to Rossadilisk right

Above: *Dr Holberton's cottage in Cleggan, showing the wireless mast.*
Opposite: *Two views of Inishbofin harbour.* (Photographs courtesy of the late Dr Evelyn Musgrave)

away to tell the fishermen not to go out. Sadly, it was already too late when Tommy, a retired naval man, headed off in great haste on his white horse. As Dr Holberton's granddaughter, the late Dr Evelyn Musgrave, pointed out when she recounted the story, if the warning had been received just an hour earlier, the tragedy might have been avoided for that particular community.

Similar warnings of a severe gale were heard by owners of wireless sets along the coast. If this information could have been conveyed to the fishermen, how many lives might have been saved? How many families would have been spared the loss of their breadwinner?

Meanwhile, over in the village of Claddaghduff, Festy Lacey was among those reciting the Rosary in the little Star-of-the-Sea church. He recalled that the wind blew up suddenly and with great ferocity, and the church was thrown into darkness as the storm obliterated the remaining light. Faces of those around him turned an eerie, ashen white as slates were ripped from the church roof. In other parts of the community, roofs were torn off cow sheds and the recently harvested hay was blown in every direction.

Above: Black Rock, the breaker near Cleggan beach, on which John Cloonan and his crew were thrown up during the storm. (Photograph courtesy of the late Dr Evelyn Musgrave)
Below: Cleggan Bay, as it appears today. (Marie Feeney)

Out on the sea, as gusts reached seventy miles per hour, the fishermen of Rossadilisk and Inishbofin were struggling for survival. John Cloonan and his crew had nearly made it to Cleggan beach that night, but landed on a breaker, known locally as Black Rock, just two hundred yards away from the shoreline. Had they gone either side of the rock, they might have been saved.

Martin Murray, Mark Lacey and the crews of their boats were lost against the rocks at Cleggan Head. John O'Halloran remembered that they were busy shooting their nets when the storm hit. There was no time to move away from the rocks, and their struggle ended as quickly as it began.

Festy Feeney and his crew were the only survivors from Rossadilisk. Using his seamanship skills, Festy battled to ride out the storm, letting his boat in and out in the sea while struggling to keep his crew

BOATS THAT LEFT ROSSADILISK

John Cloonan's boat (all lost)
John Cloonan, 46, skipper
Michael Laffey, 22
Patrick Feeney, 35
Thomas Delap, 50, married with three children
Michael Feeney, 22, brother of Patrick
Michael Cloonan, 24, son of skipper

Martin Murray's boat (all lost)
Martin Murray, 46, married with ten children between 5 and 18 years, skipper
Thomas Lacey, 26, supporter of aged parents
Michael Feeney, 21, supporter of aged parents
Patrick Davis, 40
John Murray, 40, married with 7 children

Mark Lacey's boat (all lost)
Mark Lacey, 40, skipper
Mark O'Toole, 50, married with seven children, aged between 2 and 11 years
Martin Lacey, 35, brother of skipper
George Lacey, 25, another brother
Martin Halloran

Festy Feeney's boat (the only survivors from Rossadillisk)
Festy Feeney, 44, skipper
Sheady Feeney,
Jack Murray
Martin Lacey

BOATS THAT LEFT INISHBOFIN

Pat Powell's boat (all lost)
Pat Powell, skipper
Harry Lavelle, married with a large family
Martin McHale, 24
Michael Tierney, 21
John Connolly, 20

Michael O'Toole's boat (all lost)
Michael O'Toole, 47, skipper, widowed with a young family of six children
Patrick King, 28, supporter of elderly parents
John Lavelle, 32
Thomas Scuffle, married with a family of six

Pat Concannon's boat (survivors)
Pat Concannon, skipper
William Lavelle
William Burke
Pat Burke
Mick Cloherty

Jim Cloherty's boat (survivors)
Jim Cloherty, skipper
Pat Scuffle
Martin Darcy
Peter McHale

John Scuffle's boat (survivors)
John Scuffle, skipper
Michael Kenny
Pat Scuffle
John Darcy
John Hughes

A CLEGGAN WOMAN'S LAMENT

Oh, wild and cold and cruel sea,
That keeps my love so long from me!
Alone I stand upon the shore,
And hear no voice but the ocean's roar.
My eyes are dim and my heart is sore,
Watching and waiting for you ashore.

In our little home, as I knit or spin,
I think I hear your step come in.
But it's only the wind shakes window and door.
And then goes wailing over the moor.
Then I kneel and pray to God above
To succour and save the man I love.

Oh, Michleen Oge, oh, allanna machree!
Sleep snug and safe in your cradle bed,
Though your father is out on the stormy sea.
Striving to win our daily bread,
There's One above whose word is true,
And will bring him safe to me and you.

Over the rocks the waves high,
Out on the cliffs the sea-birds cry.
The night wears through and dawn is night,
And I am still alone, achone,
My man is gone, he is young to die,
And I am left alone, mavrone.

Agnes Lynam, 1927

away from the rocks. At one stage, he attempted to take hold of his currach that was moored at Rossadilisk for ferrying the crew between the boat and the shore, but failed. The battle appeared to be lost when the tore-pin used to hold the oars broke, but in the same instant a freak wave pushed them towards the shore and threw them safely onto the beach at Sellerna. The crew wasted no time in heading for Cleggan village in order to get help and to seek news of their comrades and relatives who had gone to sea with them only a few short hours earlier.

Festy's son, Michael Feeney, recalled that his father had told him, when he was a child, about a dream that he had three weeks before the disaster. In the dream, the village was being raided by men he did not know, who stole from the inhabitants, turned their homes upside down and left the children crying. Festy awoke from the dream shouting. Was it a premonition of what was to come, and did the dream help to save his life and that of his crew? Who knows, but Festy was certain that it was an insight into what was to become of his beloved community.

The violent storm swept the boat containing Michael O'Toole and his crew onto rocks in Ballinakill harbour. His remains were later found washed ashore near Letter beach. According to reports at the time of the disaster, his body was found tied by ropes to his boat, and there were other bodies in the same area; however, by the time further help arrived, the bodies had once more been washed out to sea.

Pat Powell and his crew were lost off Inishbofin, but what exactly happened to the crew is not known. It remains one of the mysteries of that terrible night. One crew member, Martin McHale, attempted to reach Jim Cloherty's boat after the Powell boat got crushed against the rocks. His brother, Peter, who was a crew member on the Cloherty boat, reached out to save him, but Martin drowned within touching distance of Peter's hands.

Pat Concannon and his crew battled with the sea for more than six hours. Totally at the mercy of the ferocious wind, they were driven around High Island and Inishbofin, before arriving at Cleggan Pier at about three o'clock on Saturday morning. The skipper had been blinded by the saltwater spray, and all of the crew had the flesh torn from their hands by the force required to row their boat to safety.

Jim Cloherty and his crew had a narrow escape. John O'Halloran recollected that they had anchored their boat on a breaker off Inishbofin and when the storm was in full force, they tried to pull on the anchor but it would not give way. With quick thinking, Jim Cloherty cut the rope, freeing the boat from its mooring. They were then carried by the force of a wave, onto the beach at Inishbofin. After a four hour struggle, it was almost beyond belief that the entire crew was safe.

The sea was kinder to John Scuffle and his crew, who were swept to safety near Letterfrack. Having left their boat, they sent word to Cleggan to reassure their anxious families, before staying in a local farmhouse until the storm calmed down later that night.

The Inishbofin and Rossadilisk boats were not the only ones to be caught in the storm that night. John O'Halloran recollected that three small canvas currachs from the little village of Bundowlish, near Cleggan, were blown into the narrow cove known as Perth, on Cleggan Head. In the darkness, the crews were unsure of their whereabouts, but one man, Thomas Heanue, left his currach and began to climb the two hundred foot cliffs that loomed above them. Another man, named Regan, also attempted to make the climb, but slipped onto a ledge. Thomas Heanue managed to reach a nearby farmhouse, where he obtained ropes and helping hands to rescue Regan and the rest of the men trapped in the cove. Among them was Michael Mullen who, as John recalled, claimed that 'what saved him was a red scapular that a woman had given him years before.'

Opposite: *Thomas Heanue, Bundowlish* (Photograph courtesy of Essie Heanue Brown, granddaughter of Thomas Heanue)

THE SURVIVORS REMEMBER

JAMES CLOHERTY OF INISHBOFIN vividly recalled his own experience of the storm:

"We went out from Bofin before 7.00 p.m. and went fishing in East End Bay. The storm came on very suddenly and we shipped some heavy seas. I urged the men to keep rowing and to make for shore, but by this time the waves were rolling high and it was with difficulty we kept the boats ahead to the waves. We heard terrible screams and shouts in the darkness and knew that something had happened to our companions. I looked for any sign of them, but all I could see was an upturned boat going close by our own. I could see neither bodies nor signs of men in the water. Later, there were further terrible screams, and I thought we were lost ourselves as we made no headway. For twelve hours we continued to row, and at last, when we abandoned all hope, a wave threw us up safe on the Bofin beach."

John Scuffle, whose crew also went out, told a similar story. Both of these men lost their nets and considered themselves destitute. It is thought that some of those who were lost could have been saved, if they had only cut their nets in time. Keenly aware of how essential the nets were to their livelihood and what it would cost to replace them, the fishermen hung on to them until the last possible moment. One of the bodies was found enmeshed in a net – grim evidence of the efforts made to save the valuable tools of their trade.

The plight of the survivors was tragic. Fishing had not been good in the preceding years, but ironically, the season of 1927 had seen an increase in their catches and a rise in the prices paid for the fish. It

Opposite above: The East End of Inishbofin, showing the bay where the men from the island were fishing on the night of the storm. (Photograph courtesy of John Abeyta)

Opposite below: The village of Rossadilisk in 1918 (Photograph courtesy of the late Dr Evelyn Musgrave)

looked as if Inishbofin and Cleggan would enjoy a period of prosperity, but the storm deprived both communities of their best men and wage earners. Even the men who escaped said they would never venture out to fish again after their terrible experiences.

There was not a single survivor among the nine men who made up the crews of the two Bofin boats that were lost. Sixteen men were lost from Rossadilisk, with only one boat returning home. The full story of the victims' final struggle will never be known. All that is certain is that most of the crews perished in the darkness within sight of the little farmhouses that they had left a few brief hours before. The accounts given by the surviving crew from Rossadilisk suggest that the fishermen were lost in their efforts to save the nets.

A hero of the storm

The tragedy that plunged Northwest Connemara into a profound state of shock and grief was ameliorated by the heroism of Patrick Concannon, of Inishbofin, the owner of a frail tar and canvas curragh. Like the others, he set out for a night of fishing with his four man crew: Michael Cloherty, William Lavelle, William Burke, and Patrick Burke. Around 7.30 p.m., the storm struck their boat. For a while they used their nets as an anchor, but the gale was so fierce that they decided to abandon them and stand to all oars.

They were driven before the wind at enormous speed, eventually finding themselves in the lee of Davillaun Island. The force of the gale drove them past the island on the crest of gigantic waves. Trying in vain to make for the shore, they soon found themselves nine miles south of High Island.

For seven hours the boat was spun about on the inky black surface of the sea, with sleet and spray blinding the men. During the entire ordeal, Patrick Concannon remained in the bow of his curragh, shouting words of encouragement over the thunderous roar of the storm.

Around 3.00 a.m., the men were finally hurled ashore at Letter, where they lay on the beach in the scudding rain, unable to move due to hunger and severe exhaustion. They remained at Letter, which is about fifteen miles east of High Island, until they felt it was safe to leave. On Saturday afternoon, they headed for Cleggan and from there rowed back to Inishbofin, where anxious relatives waited for news of them.

Patrick Concannon (Photograph courtesy of Agatha Burke)

All members of the crew paid eloquent tribute to Patrick Concannon, to whom, in their opinions, they undoubtedly owed their lives. Such was the severity of his ordeal that those who saw Patrick on the Saturday evening reported that his hands were swollen to three times their normal size, and he had to be led about, because he had lost his ability to see. The faces and hands of the rest of the crew were also swollen, and their clothes torn to shreds.

IN MEMORIAM,
OCTOBER 28TH, 1927

Oh! wild sea, leaping madly up,
To lash, the lonely shore,
Hast thou not reaped thy meed of fame
Full measure and pressed down again,
That thou should seek for more?

The treasure of a maiden's love,
Close in thy depths you hold;
That manly form at thy behest,
Lies now upon thy chilly breast,
Within thy soft arms fold.

The crying of the fatherless,
Wails in thy waves unrest,
The widow by her lonely fire,
Yields up her loves to thy desire,
Her bravest and her best.

Tomorrow's sun shall shine, as if,
No storm winds raked the deep,
Nor children's cry, nor mother call,
Nor love's embrace avails at all,
To wake them from their sleep.

AKR, Clifden, *Connacht Tribune*, November 9th 1927

Above: *The remains of the island community at Inniskea (Inis Gé).*

Right: *The Lacken Memorial with the names of the storm's victims in Irish, presented by the people of Cleggan, Inishbofin and Lacken. In addition to those of the victims of the 1927 storm, the memorial also includes the names of two other local men lost at sea.*

Previous page: *The Cleggan Bay disaster memorial on Omey Island – a detail of the inscription appears on page 55.*

Go dtuga Dia na Glóire áit ar leith ar Neamh Dá créatúir uilig a bádhadh i gCloigeann, Inis Bó Finne, Leacain agus anseo in Inis Gé ar an 28-10-1927

Seán Ó Maoineacháin
Seán Ó Manacháin
Micheál Ó Manacháin
Mícheál Ó Catháin
Seán Ó Raghallaigh
Toirdhealbhach Ó Raghallaigh
Máirtín Ó Maoineacháin
Seán Mac Fhionntaigh
Liam Ó Raghallaigh
Seán Ó Maolfhábhail
Seán Ó Raghallaigh
Mícheál Ó Maolfhábhail

Bronnta ar Inis Gé ag muintir an Chloiginn

DISASTER AT INNISKEA
AND LACKEN BAY

Inniskea (Inis Gé) Island, County Mayo

In 1927, the odds were stacked against small fishing communities along the west coast of Ireland, and like neighbouring communities to the south, Inniskea had no lifeboats or life-saving apparatus. Three trawlers, which had been recently purchased from the French were docked at Blacksod for the winter months, due to the lack of a dock to harbour them at Inniskea. Had such facilities existed, the larger boats may have proved useful in saving lives on the night of the storm.

John and Anthony Meenaghan were among the curragh crews from Inniskea who, like those in Connemara, had set out for a night's fishing on the evening of October 28th. When the storm blew up, the two brothers used every ounce of their strength to struggle against the elements. Their curragh was tossed around by the angry, churning sea until they were finally driven ashore onto the beach at Tirrane and Aughleam, a distance of about five miles from the island. By then it was about nine o'clock.

The other crews were less fortunate, although at one time they came within a short distance of landing at Inniskea. They battled heroically against the tempest. Blinded by the spray that was whipped up in the westerly gale, they struggled in vain to maintain control of their boats. Their nets, laden with mackerel, were snatched away by the sea and later washed up on Tirrane and Aughleam.

The body of William Reilly was taken to Blacksod, where it lay until the following Sunday in the house of a man named Michael Keane, awaiting interment at Faulmore, the nearest graveyard to the islands. Despite a boisterous sea, grieving relatives of the deceased and missing crews made the journey to Blacksod to wake and bury their dead companion.

Lacken Bay

Sorrow also stalked through the fishing village of Lacken, in northwest Mayo, where the sea claimed the lives of nine men.

Bodies Found in Mayo

Early on Sunday, 27th November, the bodies of two victims of the Inniskea fishing disaster were found near Blacksod. The burials took place after Mass in the cemetery at Faulmore, alongside those of their late comrades. Father Dodd, P.P., read the burial service. The bodies could not be identified, but two islanders who crossed to the mainland recognised the clothing as that of Martin Meenaghan and John Monaghan. The bodies of two more of the victims of the Western tragedy were washed ashore during the week, one at Cross near Binghamstown, and one at Blacksod. They were identified as those of Willie O'Reilly, North Island and John Monaghan, South Island. The body of John McGinty was recovered on Friday.

A VISIT TO THE INISKEA ISLANDS

An article by Sir John Lumsden, a member of the National Relief Fund Committee, originally written for the Irish Independent

Sir John Lumsden (Photograph courtesy of the *Irish Independent*)

In the following article, specially written for the *Irish Independent*, a visit to some of the sufferers of the terrible disasters to fishing boats off the West Coast last October is described. Light is thrown upon the hard lot of these industrious but ill-fed and poorly-housed people, and upon what is being done by the West Coast Disaster National Relief Fund to alleviate their plight, while remedies are suggested which might rescue them permanently from the pathetic conditions under which they live.

Leaving Ballycroy, a village 12 miles north of Mallaranny, made famous in Maxwell's classic, *Wild Sports in the West*, 1832, we proceeded through the vast bog lands flanked by the Nephin range of hills, then crossing the Owenmore River at Bangor Erris, we ran to Belmullet – a tidy and busy little village for such a poverty-stricken district as Mayo.

Turning south along the peninsula we reached Blacksod, passing on our left the ancient Bingham's Castle and the whaling station, which is being equipped again after a lapse of eight years or so. Norwegians are in charge of the reconstruction, and it is hoped the venture will prove both remunerative and a source of local employment next year.

A Beautiful Bay

Blacksod Bay is a most striking sheet of water, splendidly sheltered and picturesque, bounded by Achill-Slievemore standing up in all its grandeur, and under its shadow, Dugort. The Bay is deep, and possesses anchorage for a fleet; indeed, the late Lord Fisher once declared it was the finest natural harbour in the British Isles and capable of containing the entire Navy.

In the village of Blacksod, we met the Most Reverend Dr. Naughton, Bishop of Killala, a gracious, kindly-hearted prelate, who thoroughly understands the mentality of the fisherfolk and their needs. We discussed the problem of the Inniskea islanders and the dependents of the poor men drowned in the greatest storm last October. Crossing the hill, we came to the ancient village of Fallmore, which faces Iniskea Island, Duvillaun More and Beg, the Bull Rock in the distance.

So that these poor people could start again, and accommodate themselves to the altered circumstances. The Irish peasant, although ignorant and perhaps superstitious, has a very keen business sense, parts with money slowly, and generally gets good value for it.

Later grants

Later on, capitation grants will be given to widows and dependents, and the children will receive allowances till they attain an earning age.

Thus, a kindly public may be assured that these poor people will not materially suffer, and the money so generously entrusted to the Committee will be properly dispensed and used to the best possible advantage.

Cabin 200 years old, a pitiable sight

I took a photograph of a stone cabin reputed to be close upon 200 years old, and still occupied by an old man and his sister. It is hardly conceived that human beings could exist in such a house – no beds, just straw, the fireplace at the end, and the chimney a hole in the roof. The hens and the goat occupy one end of the habitation, and no doubt, if the resident had a cow and a pig, they would also share the house.

A Sick Girl

I was pressed to enter another adjacent cottage to see a sick girl, whom I examined. She was lying in one of those beds built into the wall, enveloped in numerous blankets about six times heavier than necessary. Her head and face were entirely covered up, and her wasted frame enclosed in coarse flannel garments. She was sweating profusely and no wonder! She was recovering from pleuro-pneumonia, and doing her utmost to fight tuberculosis.

I have examined many sick peasants in Co. Mayo, and have invariably found similar conditions – no air, no light, and a vitiated, utterly unhealthy atmosphere. It is a strange anomaly that these people, who live in such pure and sweet air all day long, should spend half of their existence in the most unhygienic and absolutely unhealthy surroundings.

It is, therefore, not surprising that tuberculosis is rife, anaemia common, and convalescence always slow. If this ignorance of the laws of hygiene could be overcome by education, how healthy these people might in time become!

Peaceful resting place

We next visited, just above the shore, a little cemetery where nine of the victims of the fishing disaster were buried in one grave marked by a roughly cut cross. A peaceful resting place, looking out on the broad Atlantic which supported them, but finally claimed them for its own in one of its angry humours.

Our party now boarded two curraghs used for fishing – frail structures made of a few boards covered with canvas and tarred over. How these boats stand up to the Atlantic gales is a marvel!

Pathetic state of things

The islands of Inniskea, north and south are about five miles distant, each island having on it about twenty-five cottages. The conditions there are truly pathetic. The islands are composed of clay, sand and

*A currach of the type used by the Inniskea fishermen. (*Photograph courtesy of the *Irish Independent)*

rock, without a foot of bog, and, consequently, all fuel has to bought on the mainland. The cottages are broken down, dark, airless-looking and damp. Corrugated iron or zinc roofs, which are mostly worn away, take the place of the old fashioned thatch. The fishermen are a hardy, weather-beaten crowd – the women and children mostly unhealthy looking, anaemic, ricketty, and under nourished. Their diet is largely composed of tea, bread, and potatoes, a very little milk and butter occasionally, and no green vegetables, but of course, fish always – a diet dangerously short of vitamins, fats, and proteins.

The Great Tragedy

I now attained my chief object, namely, to interrogate the survivors of the victims of the storm. They told me that on October 28th thirty curraghs went out to fish in the smooth sea. A westerly gale sprang up about seven o'clock with extraordinary suddenness. The lucky ones pulled for shelter of the island, or cut their nets away and bolted for shore, but six or eight curraghs – each manned by two men – were swamped, some of the crews being entangled in their nets, while one or two boats were driven on the mainland, the occupants being dashed upon the rocks.

Two bedraggled fishermen struggled through the storm to the village of Fallmore to acquaint the cottagers with the fate of their comrades. The storm lasted for a fortnight, no communication with the islands was possible, and during one week 9 bodies were washed up on the shore, and were buried in the little cemetery without the presence of one member of their families at the funerals.

148 Dependents

The feelings of these unfortunate families can be pictured – their dear ones dead, and their means of livelihood all gone. Forty-five men were drowned at Inniskea, Lacken, Inishbofin and Cleggan, leaving behind them 148 dependents. The country was shocked, relief funds were quickly organised by the Press, and President Cosgrave appointed a Committee to deal with the West Coast Disaster National Relief Fund. A sum of £36,000 was collected, many substantial subscriptions coming from America, Australia and the Colonies.

The circumstances of each family have been most carefully looked into. The local clergy have been active in their inquiries, and their advice has been helpful. The Archbishop of Tuam and the Bishop of Killala, with Mr. John Healy, have been the most energetic members of the Committee, and have taken the greatest trouble to ascertain how best relief can be given.

A clean slate

As a first step, after the immediate needs of the victims were attended to the sum of £100 was allocated to each family. It was found that most of these were in debt to local traders, and although it seemed undesirable to take this into account, it was felt that it would be wise to wipe the slate clean.

The fishing industry

I returned to our fishing lodge with two visions of the future in my mind. The first is that of the establishment of a remunerative fishing industry along this coast, with all its infinite possibilities of development, if proper harbours, up-to-date boats and nets were available, and a market for the fishermen's catches provided by a daily service of motor boats for the collection of the herrings, mackerel, turbot, cod, sole, lobsters, crab, etc., which abound in these waters.

It seems to me an effort should be made to educate the fisher folk to carry out modern methods and get away from the traditional and old-fashioned way of fishing. This surely Ministry of Fisheries should do.

Blacksod Bay

The second vision – the utilisation of Blacksod Bay as a packet station. Either Galway or Blacksod would form the shortest route for Americans coming to Great Britain and the Continent, and what a boon that would be for this beautiful land, with its fine peasants, its picturesque scenery, and its natural harbours.

Then would cease the emigration of the best blood of the West to the States, and the annual visits to Scotland for "pratie digging," which form the chief source of income for the Achill men and other islanders on the Connaught coast, who cannot make a living off their stony, boggy farmlets.

INNISKEA FISHERMEN LOST

William Reilly, 19
John McGinty, 21
Martin Meenaghan, 23, sole supporter of aged parents
John Meenaghan, married with 7 children
Michael Monaghan, 28
John Reilly, survived by parents, 2 young brothers and 3 sisters
Terence Reilly, 16
Michael Monaghan, 33, survived by aged parents and an invalid brother
Michael Keane, 18, survived by an elderly father, one brother and a sister
John Reilly, 21

LACKEN BAY FISHERMEN LOST

Thomas Lynott, 48, married with 2 children
Patrick Kearney, 40, married
Martin Kearney, 34, Patrick's brother, supporter of 2 invalid sisters
Thomas Goldrick, 40, ex-navy man, survivor of the battles of Jutland and Zeebrugge.
Anthony Goldrick, 31, nephew of Thomas, sole supporter of mother and 3 children
Anthony Coolican, 21, lived with sisters and 2 brothers
Michael Goldrick, 34
Patrick Goldrick, 19, brother of Michael
Anthony Kearney, 30, sole supporter of sister

The Murray children – among the orphans of the Cleggan Bay disaster.
(Photograph courtesy of the *Irish Independent*)

THE DAYS THAT FOLLOWED

THE FOLLOWING ACCOUNTS are based on extracts from the country edition of the *Connacht Tribune* of November 5th 1927. Memories have inevitably faded and much information was not recorded in full by those who were left behind, but the papers provided good coverage of the disaster and its aftermath. At the time there was a great deal of confusion surrounding the events of that terrible night, especially regarding deaths and the recovery of bodies, but during my research, newspaper accounts proved to be invaluable in helping to portray the story as accurately as possible.

The all night search

Sergeant Thomas O'Leary, a guard from Cleggan, in an interview at the time, said that 'it was reported at the barracks that the fishermen had gone out to sea'. He and a party of guards took lamps and went down to Cleggan quay. While they searched along the shoreline, a report came to them that a body had been found half buried in the sand further along the beach at Cleggan. The body was later identified as that of John Cloonan.

The search continued all night, but the guards saw no further signs of either the men or their boats. At 12 noon on Saturday, two more bodies were found at Letterfrack.

By the time the *Connacht Tribune* correspondent arrived in Cleggan on the Saturday evening, the storm had abated but rain was falling softly and without intermission. In the darkness, the crying of the women and children welled up and was lost in the waves of the bay beneath whose dark waters many of their husbands, fathers, brothers and sons lay. Light shone at intervals along the shoreline as the search was continued from rock to rock and from cove to cove.

In the little hall opposite the only provision shop in the village, in five pitch pine coffins, the remains of the fishermen whose bodies had been recovered lay side by side. Relatives came and prayed and wept, and then faded into the mist.

Some of the families had been left without a male breadwinner. The Revd. Eamon O'Malley, Catholic curate of Claddaghduff, who had not had a wink of sleep for 36 hours, received the newspaper's correspondent in silence. He was so overcome by the disaster, the worst in living memory on the Connemara coast, that he was unable to speak for a moment.

He led the reporter to the five coffins. 'People say,' he murmured, as they bowed their heads beside those who wept and prayed, 'that the Connemara fishermen are lazy and they do not venture out to sea to fish. These poor people with their couple of acres had either to fish or starve.'

The two men passed out into the night, while the searchers moved away with their lights through the rock and sea wrack, hoping against hope to find some loved one or neighbour who had gone so cheerfully from the little community a few hours before.

Search continued Saturday and Sunday

All through Friday night, Saturday and Sunday the search continued. There was a painful scene at about one o'clock on Sunday morning when John S. Conroy, the coroner from the West Riding of Galway, arrived in Cleggan, and the coffin lids were raised momentarily in order that the relatives could identify the remains.

Three candles lit the little hall where the villagers had intended to hold a ceili that night. Instead, their friends and neighbours lay there in the eerie light. After identities were established, the coroner gave an order for burial and announced that the inquest would be held on Monday.

The inquest

The coroner, J.S. Conroy, held an inquest in Cleggan on the following Monday afternoon. Representing the gardai were Chief Superintendent McManus, Galway, and Superintendent Allen, Clifden. After evidence was given regarding identification, witnesses gave their accounts of finding the bodies.

A typical fisherman's cottage in the west of Ireland at the time of the disaster.
(Photograph courtesy of the *Irish Independent*)

Patrick Feeney, an elderly man of 76, told a pitiful story. Two of his family – his son, Michael, and son-in-law, Martin – had been out in the storm. Martin had been saved, but there was no news of Michael.

'I was looking for my son, sir,' Feeney told the coroner. 'I was looking for my poor boy along the beach on Saturday. I had come as far as Cleggan quay after searching everywhere, and I saw a hand up out of the water. I went down and partly pulled in the body, but I had to get assistance before I could see who it was. When help came, I learned that the body was that of Thomas Delap and I had not yet found my poor son.'

In answer to questions from Superintendent McManus, witnesses said that each of the boats that were lost would have been carrying seven nets, which would weigh about two hundredweight each. When taken in from the water, the nets occupied a good deal of space and sometimes hampered the oarsmen. There was no rudder or tiller of any kind on the light, frail vessels.

Dr Michael Lavelle, Letterfrack, gave medical evidence. He was given permission to make a statement outside the medical testimony. In the absence of a jury, he said that he wished to convey to the proper authorities the criminal folly of people being compelled to go out to sea in crafts that would not be used as pleasure crafts, even in good weather. In order to get the necessities of life, these men had no choice but to use the boats. He recalled the time when there was as fine a fleet of good fishing boats to be seen in Cleggan as would be found in any part of Ireland.

The coroner, who brought in a verdict of accidental drowning, said that he had seen some of the boats and could not endorse them. All of the men who had been found had been the sole support of their families, and one man had left ten young children.

A deputation of relatives of the deceased stated that they wished to have recorded their appreciation of the great effort made by Dr Lavelle and Sergeant O'Leary, along with the guards in Cleggan and Letterfrack, on behalf of the men who had lost their lives.

Reactions at home and abroad

The whole country was deeply disturbed by the Cleggan disaster. In Irish circles in the United States, where many of the relatives and friends of the victims earned their living, news of the tragedy evoked keen regret and sympathy. The story of the disaster told by the *Connacht Tribune's* special correspondents created a painful sensation when it was given by them to the world, and funds poured in for the relief of those who had been bereaved.

The *Connacht Tribune's* special correspondent at Cleggan reported that, in response to the disaster and the desperate plight of the communities involved, the Department of Fisheries would provide suitable boats, of a safe type, for fishermen for the next season. It was understood that Scottish fish skewers would be brought over for the next herring season and by these means it was hoped that fishing could be put on a sound basis in the area.

After Gerald Bartley of Clifden brought the disaster to the notice of the members of Galway County Council, they passed a resolution of sympathy and suggested that the government take steps to provide the Western fishermen with better gear.

Two Irish Air Force planes flown by Cpt. Crossley and Cpt. Heron reached the western bay and islands to aid in the search for those still missing after the tragedy.

A common form of transport in the west of Ireland in the 1920s. (Photograph courtesy of the *Irish Independent*)

Touching tributes

All the masses in the district on Sunday morning were offered for the repose of the souls of the brave men who had been lost in the storm. An ailing Monsignor McAlpine rose from his bed that morning, against the advice of his doctors to officiate at mass in Claddaghduff church. He told the congregation that the hearts of all went out in the most profound sense to those who had lost relatives and friends in this terrible catastrophe at sea. Joining with the mourners in their sorrow, he asked the congregation to pray for them and asked Almighty God to take care of the bereaved and stricken families who had lost their breadwinners in the disaster.

Father O'Malley, the Catholic curate of the district, broke down at the steps of the altar as he tried to offer a word of sympathy, and every member of his congregation was in tears.

The Reverend John Burke CC celebrated mass at Ballinakill church for the repose of the souls of all who had been taken from them so suddenly in the night. He urged worshippers to support their neighbours who had been left alone and without help. He spoke of the need for all those who go down to the sea in ships to earn their living always to be prepared to meet their God. Who could have known that a storm would come so suddenly upon these men who put out to sea to pursue their livelihood? Who could have known that death was waiting for them in the bay that they knew so well?

Archbishop's References

Speaking at St Jarlath's Cathedral on Sunday, the Archbishop, the Most Reverend Dr Kilmartin, asked for sympathy, prayers and practical charity for 'the victims of the awful disaster on the Connemara coast'. He had wired his 'profound sympathy and willingness to help in relieving the acute deprivation, which the disaster is bound to entail' and sent the sum of 50 pounds to Fr O'Malley for relief purposes. He stated that he felt sure that the public would co-operate with the government in bringing relief to the dependants of the 25 breadwinners, who had sacrificed their lives to provide for their families.

A common grave

On Sunday afternoon, a sad little procession moved the five coffins from the hall in Cleggan to the picturesque Stella Maris (Star-of-the-Sea) church, three miles away in Claddaghduff. There the coffins remained overnight as silent mourners passed in and out, stopping to kneel and pray and to kiss the coffin lids.

High mass was held at Claddaghduff for the deceased men on Monday. Michael O'Toole's body was then taken to Cleggan pier, and conveyed from there to Inishbofin on the *O'Morochue*. The bodies of the other four fishermen were taken to Omey Island, where they were buried in a common grave. The heart-rending sound of weeping women and children filled the air, and the realisation that the bodies of some of the men might never be recovered only made their sorrow worse.

Speaking after High Mass on Monday, Fr Edward O'Malley CC, Cleggan, asked once again for prayers to be offered for those who had perished in such tragic circumstances. He stated with conviction that, although their call was sudden, the men had prepared their souls for God. Having lived the poor man's difficult struggle to survive, the men had surely earned the poor man's beatitude, he felt.

'This I say,' said Fr O'Malley, '. . . that it is sad to think that in any Christian land, men must risk their lives, or face starvation for themselves and their families. It is sadder still to think that it needs a tragedy to arouse in the minds of the authorities, the consciousness of the terrible reality of the poor man's struggle for existence. These men have left behind them destitute relations, parents bogged down with age and children of tender years.'

Islanders' Grief: Arrival of the O'Morochue at Bofin

At about 1.00 p.m. on Saturday, the Free State patrol boat *O'Morochue* arrived at Cleggan and M.J. Mongan T.D., Mr. McQuillan, Coast Saving Service, Sergeant O'Leary, Cleggan and a civic guard went on board and the boat set out on the six miles journey to Inishbofin. As a small boat, which put off from the *O'Morochue* came near, the islanders crowded along the shore, eagerly awaiting news of the life or death of their people.

News of their safety would mean life, no news could not mean anything but death. 'What is the news from the mainland?' they asked. Reluctantly they were informed that there was no news of the men. On hearing this, the women collapsed in grief, having waited there since Friday night, some of them hoping against hope for good news.

The majority of the women, however seemed to feel that it was useless to hope for news of survivors and were already mourning for them as lost. The islanders who had reached Cleggan on Friday night had returned when the sea grew calm but they had heard by then that Michael O'Toole's body had been found, and knew, beyond reasonable doubt that the other members of his crew could not have survived. Nevertheless, they clung to the hope that some men might be safe and this had only tended to increase the general feeling of tension among the relatives.

More bodies recovered

The ordeal continued for the families and friends of the victims, as bodies were washed up along the shoreline in the weeks following the storm. On Sunday, November 6th, the body of Patrick Feeney (27), of Rossadilisk, was washed ashore at Cleggan beach, close to where some of the other bodies were recovered immediately after the storm.

At about eight o'clock that morning, two members of the civic guards, Sergeant O'Leary and Guard Keohane, were patrolling along the coast, on the lookout for any bodies of the victims that might be thrown up by the sea. It was expected that, by that stage, nine days after the tragedy, some of the bodies would be recovered. The Guards noticed what appeared to be the body of a man floating in the tide near the shore. They waded out and brought the corpse onto the land.

Although the face was disfigured beyond recognition, the man was subsequently identified by his father from the clothes he was wearing. The body was put into a coffin and placed in the same shed where, one week before, rested the remains of the five fishermen whose bodies were washed ashore when the storm subsided.

Patrick Feeney was one of the crew on John Cloonan's boat, who went out to fish from Rossadilisk on the ill-fated night. Their boat was lost and the whole crew perished. Another member of the crew, Martin O'Halloran, was still missing.

The coroner was again notified, but he did not consider an inquest necessary. Later in the afternoon, the remains were taken to the Star-of-the-Sea Church, Claddaghduff, where they were received by the Reverend O'Malley, C.C.

The same sad spectacle of the previous Sunday was again witnessed when the remains of the other victims were buried.

Ten days later, on Wednesday, November 16th, another body was washed up near Cleggan. and was identified as that of Martin O'Halloran, of Rossadilisk. O'Halloran, who was unmarried, was the remaining member of the crew of John Cloonan's boat, and his body was the seventh to be recovered out of the total loss of twenty-five lives.

On Monday, 28th November, the body of John Murray, a married man of about 40 years from Rossadilisk, was found washed ashore on an uninhabited island called Innishbroon, situated about a mile off the Connemara coast at Renvyle. The discovery was made by Thomas O'Malley of Cashleen, Renvyle, who went to the island in search of seaweed, used in the making of kelp. He reported the matter immediately to the civic guards at Letterfrack, and later a party from Rossadilisk proceeded to the spot to identify the body.

THOMAS DELAP

ON THE SOULS OF
JOHN KING   MARTIN KING

MARTIN HOLLERAN. MARK LACEY.
PATRICK FEENEY. GEORGE LACEY.
MARTIN MURRAY. MARTIN LACEY.
MICHAEL FEENEY. THOMAS WALSH.
PATRICK DAVIS.   JOHN MURRAY.
MICHAEL FEENEY   THOMAS LACEY.
JOHN CLOONAN. MARK TOOLE.
WHO LOST THEIR LIVES IN CLEGGAN BAY
ON 20ᵗʰ OCTOBER 1927.
SWEET JESUS HAVE MERCY.
R. I. P.

Above: The memorial stone on Omey Island with the names of those who died in the storm on October 28th 1927.
Below, left to right: Austin Kelly, John O'Halloran and Patrick Concannon.

The remains were placed in a coffin and conveyed late on Tuesday evening to Claddaghduff Church, where the Reverend E. O'Malley, C.C. once again performed the sad task of receiving the body.

Mass was celebrated the following day by Father O'Malley, after which the funeral took place at the little churchyard on the edge of Omey island. The coffin was placed side by side with the other victims of the disaster whose bodies had already been recovered.

John Murray was a member of the crew of Martin Murray's boat. He left a wife and seven young children.

A WESTERN DISASTER

There are heart thrills of deep bitter anguish,
In the homes of the fishermen brave,
Who perished on the 28th of October
Beneath the Atlantic's wild wave.
It shocked the whole world with its horror,
When the news spread around on the day
Of the awful disaster that happened
In Cleggan and Lacken and poor Inniskea.

How jovial their minds and contented
While skillfully sorting their old torn gear,
Hoping to land some small catches
Of fish that were temptingly near.
Signs of storm appeared, but they ventured
To gather a crust from the sea,
All other resources denied them
In a wilderness far from being free.

The storm in aspect appalling
Arose frantically raging its might,
Sweeping its victims before it,
To perilous rocks foaming white
In wrath the elements trembled,
Mocking weird was the gloom
That enveloped the gallant sea toilers
Hurriedly forced to their doom.

Mrs John Murray with her seven children ranging in age from 2 to 11 years.
(Photograph courtesy of the *Irish Independent*)

Its work of destruction soon ended,
Leaving ruin and despair in its track,
The caoine on the scene was heart rending,
For the brave who failed to come back.
In the grip of unfettered affliction
Their kindred incessantly moan,
All joy from their lives is extinguished,
Sad, tearful and cheerless their home.

Our sympathy sincere and unstinted
Towards the subjects of sorrow now flow,
Of all those bereaved by the storm
In Galway and in Co. Mayo.
May the souls of the men who departed
In the rage of the storm that night
Be resplendent in the mansions of glory,
Surrounded by Christ's beaming light.

William Burns, Portacloy, Broadhaven.
(First published in the *Mayo News*)

FROM THE NEWSPAPERS

LOCAL AND NATIONAL NEWSPAPERS carried a wide variety of articles, stories and letters concerning the west coast calamities. The following are a selection of these, and may help to reflect the reactions to the disaster at the time. I am grateful to the newspapers for allowing me to reprint these.

A VISIT TO ROSSADILISK

A correspondent from the *Irish Independent* visited the village of Rossadilisk the evening after the storm. His report tells of a community devastated by the tragedy:

I visited that little stricken village of Rossadilisk this evening. It was an unnerving experience, for it meant wading through misery. There are about 20 houses in the village. To a dozen of them the angel of death has come and called away some loved one. From one house three have gone; from two others two each have gone; in all sixteen valued lives are lost.

From the sturdy father of ten, to the beardless youth who had just passed his teens, suddenly, ruthlessly, the mysterious sea demanded its toll.

And here is the terrible bitterness of the awful tragedy, the sea has not given up its dead. The sea still holds 12, and this evening when I visited that place it seemed to me as if it were trying to guard its secret jealously. There was naught to break the silence save the roar of a crashing wave, or the cry of a wild sea fowl.

Opposite, top: *Mrs Mark O'Toole, widow of one of the fishermen, with her five children, in the single room which their housing comprised.*
Opposite, bottom: *Mrs Martin Murray with nine of her ten children, who were left without a father as a result of the storm.* (Photographs courtesy of the *Irish Independent*)

There are boats along by the strand. Some are out in the bay. Two of the latter are upside down; the others are half submerged. There are few men left in the village to attend to them, and in those who are left the sea has inspired so great a dread that they do nothing but gaze into it with eyes that reflect awe and fear.

Father O'Malley, a young man at that time, showed the journalist around and this is what he saw.

I was brought into the houses of the afflicted ones. In the dozen houses there are a few old men, many pale faced women with eyes re-rimmed with bitter tears, and about a score of children, from the gurgling babe at its mothers breast to the full grown youth conscious of the tragedy, which makes him the boy head of the house.

In the homes

There was one I visited which recalled the worst days of stricken Connemara. A long, low-roofed cabin, without a window even, a chimney reeking with turf smoke.

As the place was, I had to pause for a minute until my eyes got accustomed to the gloom. Inside the door a calf, and to the left, a dog eating its miserable feed, and fowls all around the house. There was a woman there, nursing a baby, and huddled in a corner near the turf fire four other children all of tender years. This woman's husband, the father of those helpless, innocent babies, had gone down in the sea. This was the worst house, but the others were not much better. It was the only one in which I saw livestock. Just a few of them would pass as comfortable habitations – comfortable, that is, when judged by the prevailing standard of a district where the degree of life is low.

I was brought into all those houses, rarely have I seen such terrible grief, some bear the blow bravely, but hard. Others have gone down crushed with sorrow. I saw one poor creature almost demented. Her only hope and help, her brother, was lost. She was alone, all alone, in the world. How she cried and wailed to the heart bruised young priest; how she clung to him and prayed to the good God to send another storm, that the sea would bring back her dead.

Then there was the poor mother who lost her three sons. One of them, the best and bravest of them all, her son Mark, the eldest of the three, he who was looked upon as one of the best fishermen and

APPALLING IRISH
CATASTROPHES

FISHING FLEETS SUNK OFF WEST COAST

FIFTY PERSONS PERISH

AGONIZING SCENES IN GALWAY AND MAYO

THE PRESIDENT'S SYMPATHY

GREAT BRITAIN—Dead 19
OTHER FATAL CASUALTIES 3

TOTAL 73

This is the appalling death roll which resulted from the fierce storm on Friday night. Three awful disasters occurred to fishing fleets off the coasts of Galway and Mayo, in which the number of persons that perished is, according to the latest information available, 51.

ablest seaman on this stretch of coast; he who had gone down to the sea for years; knew it and met it in its every mood, and ever claimed the victory. Well might that poor afflicted mother say to the comforting priest: "It was a bad sea that took my Mark, Father". She bears her terrible trial bravely, but ever and again she cries out in her misery, exclaiming; "Oh where are my three fine boys?". You leave that house with something in your throat, and there is a resounding crash of a broken wave, a sound that is like into demoniacal laughter; the gloating of the sea over its bloody prey. You go into the next house. It must have been a happy home. This evening there were two widows there and ten orphans. He who is lost kept his widowed mother with his wife and ten children. What pretty children they are – five boys and five girls. There must have been six of them in that group sitting on the hearth.

'And how greedy he was for us all, father' said the mother in that wonderfully expressive way of saying she had lost a good husband and father.

These little children looked as if they were well provided for. Blissfully ignorant of their awful fate, they looked at you, their big bright eyes filled with wonder and surprise as if they were trying to pierce the veil of innocence, and yet at that thing that brought those terrible tears to their mother's eyes. On to another house where the father had gone, leaving a widow and seven helpless children, but why continue this tragic journey? Why pursue this weary road of grief? It was the same story in every house from Rossadilisk to Bofin and around the Mayo coast.

SISTER'S SAD PLIGHT *(newspaper report 26/11/27)*
Brother lost in the fishing disaster – Cow disposed of to buy food
The body of Martin O'Halloran (single), of Rossadilisk, one of the victims of the recent fishing disaster, which was washed ashore on Cleggan strand, makes the seventh body recovered out of the total number of twenty-five lives lost from Rossadilisk and Inishbofin.

The discovery was made by Guard Edward Cantwell, who is stationed at Clogheen, Co. Tipperary, and was home on leave with his relatives, who reside in the immediate neighbourhood. He has conveyed word to the Civic Guards at Cleggan, and Sergeant O' Leary and Guard Keohane were promptly on the spot. The body was in an advanced state of de-composition, but the man was identified by a jersey he was wearing. The remains were immediately coffined and convoyed to the little church at Claddaghduff. The Coroner for the West Riding, Mr. J. S. Conroy, solicitor, Galway, was at once communicated with, but he did not consider an inquest necessary.

The funeral took place on Thursday morning to Omey, and the body was placed side by side with those of the other victims whose bodies have already been recovered.

O'Halloran was one of the crew of John Cloonan's boat, all of whom have now been accounted for. He leaves a sister to mourn his loss. They lived together in an humble cottage in the village of Rossadilisk, their only assets being two acres of barren ground, two cows and a calf, and Martin's share as a member of the crew of the ill-fated boat, which was lost in the storm. This is a particularly sad case, in as much as the unfortunate sister is now left alone in the world, without visible means of subsistence. She was obliged to part with one of her cows since her brother was lost in order to get a few pounds to help to keep the wolf from the door. This case is only typical as showing the great distress which already exists amongst the bereaved families in Rossadilisk.

The Civic Guards are continuing their searches along the coast in the hope of finding some of the bodies of the other victims.

MR. COSGRAVE AND THE SCHOOLBOYS

(Irish Independent)

President Cosgrave's visit to the United States will be watched with interest by the pupils of Bembridge School, in the Isle of Wight. The lads were among the earliest to respond to his appeal on behalf of the Western Distress Fund, and the President, with characteristic kindness, sent them a personal letter of thanks, which is published in the autumn issue of the school's newspaper – written and edited by members of the school, and printed by them at the Yellowsands Press, the private press of Bembridge School.

'My dear boys,' says Mr. Cosgrave, 'I have received your generous subscription to the National Fund for the immediate relief of the many dependents of the victims of the recent tragedy on the coasts of Galway and Mayo and to make such future provisions for them as may be necessary. I desire to express to you the very sincere thanks of the Committee and myself for your generous response to the national appeal. It is a source of great satisfaction to us to receive your donation so promptly, as it indicates that you have a real and practical sympathy for the stricken families on these wild and isolated seaboards.'

Yours sincerely,

W.T. Cosgrave.

A SCHOOLGIRL'S IMPRESSION OF A GREAT SORROW

The first prize of one guinea was awarded by the *Connacht Sentinel* in its Christmas writing competition in 1927 to Mary King from Moyard National School, Connemara. It went as follows:

The sad news which spread quickly, brought a sigh to many a heart. All were anxious to sympathise with the bereaved relatives. On the day of the funeral of those whose bodies had been recovered, many people flocked to the picturesque little church where high Mass was being celebrated for the repose of the souls of those who had perished.

I do not live many miles from the scene of the disaster, and I attended the funeral in company with a friend. The October wind was sighing through the trees. The sea, which had been so cruel only a few days before was calm and still. The sun bathed the entire landscape in glowing colours. The lakes and ponds which were filled by the recent rain showed silver surfaces. It was a scene of beauty so complete as to carry with it a sense of sadness.

As I neared the little church in which the bodies lay, sad scenes met my eyes. People were visiting the church, some of them being those who were bereaved and the wailing of the women and children was heart rending, so much so that for weeks afterwards I imagined I could hear it. On entering the church, where four pine coffins lay, I knelt at the end of the seat next to the door, I could not bear to look where they were. One glance I got at the heart broken relatives kneeling in silent prayer beside the coffins of their loved ones told me how terrible were their feelings.

As the priest ascended the altar a great silence fell on the congregation. All were crushed with sorrow. The priest offered up the August Sacrifice of Calvary for the victims of the terrible disaster. When the Mass was over he spoke a few words of comfort to those who were left behind in a cold and cheerless world. When at last the time came for leaving the church, the four coffins were taken out and carried down the church. As they passed out, followed by the sorrowing friends, it was a scene pathetic in the extreme. Slowly the procession moved towards the little churchyard of Omey, which has the sea on three sides of it. As I came in sight of the sea which had claimed them as victims I could not find that rapture by its shore or "Music in its roar" as Lord Byron did.

The churchyard of Omey, which was formerly an island, is situated about three miles from the little village in which the fishermen lived. It is surrounded by water when there is a high tide. The passage to it is merely the sand drifted in by the sea. On this island Saint Feichin founded a Monastery in about the sixth century, but like all old Monastic buildings which flourished during Ireland's "gold age", it is now a ruin, nothing remaining but a few slabs to mark the spot where that ancient Monastery once stood.

The present graveyard stands on the site of the old Monastic ruins. When the funeral procession reached it, the four coffins were laid side by side, I hope I shall never again behold such a sight. To see the poor people whose friends had been taken on that terrible night by the cruel sea was enough to make the hardest hearts fill with sorrow. Little did any of those whose bodies had been laid to rest in the holy soils of Omey think of death a week before that day. After one night they were no more.

Slowly and sadly we left the graveside with the picture we had seen vividly before the mind's eye. No tragedy that was witnessed in recent years could be more heart breaking than this. As we left, the beauty of the scenery about seemed a mockery. No bright ray could dispel the darkness that seemed to have fallen on the whole locality.

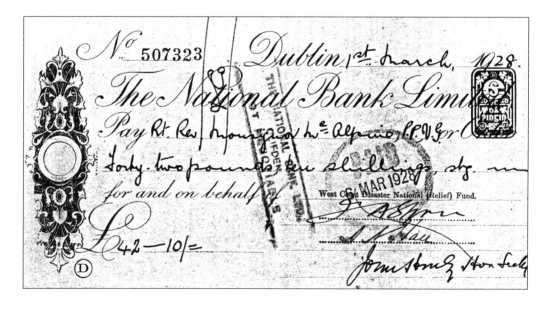

Telegrafa an Phuist.

Ní mór an fhuirm seo do chur le h-aon fhiafruí a déanfar mar gheall ar an telegram so.
(This form must accompany any enquiry respecting this telegram.)

Oifig Tosnuithe agus Treoracha Seirbhíse.

Clifden 14

Táille le n-íoc
(To Pay)

Síneadh isteach ar a
(Handed in at) 3.24 P M.   Fachta annso ar a
(Received here at) 3-32. P M.

Do
(TO)

President Cosgrave
An Dáil Dublin
Will act on your committee
most heartily
Monsignor McAlpine

Foghluim Gaedhilg, cabruigh le cleasa lúith na nGael, agus cuidigh le Saothar Gaolach. Cuir do chuid airgid i mBanco an Phuist. Bíodh Teletón agat.

Learn Irish, foster Irish games and support Irish industries. Put your savings into the Post Office Bank. Instal a Telephone.

Above: *Telegram sent to President Cosgrave by Monsignor McAlpine*
Below: *Cheque sent to Monsignor McAlpine from the West Coast Disaster Relief Fund.* (Facimiles courtesy of the National Archives, Dublin)

No 507323   Dublin 1st March, 1928.

The National Bank Limited

Pay Rt. Rev Monsignor Wm Alpine P.P. V Gr

Forty two pounds ten shillings stg

for and on behalf of   West Coast Disaster National (Relief) Fund.

£42 — 10/=

John Stone Hon Secy

OFFICIAL RESPONSES

Telegrams received

As soon as President Cosgrove heard of the tragedy, he telephoned his heart-felt sympathy to Monsignor McAlpine and informed him that he had asked the Aran lifeboat and SSM *Morochue* to proceed to Cleggan. The *Morochue,* with Captain Thompson, had been at Galway Docks, and arrived at Cleggan on Sunday afternoon. From there it proceeded immediately to Inishbofin with Mr. McQuillian of the Coast Life Saving Service, who had arrived at Cleggan on Saturday evening, and a number of civic guards aboard.

General O'Duffy, the chief commissioner of the civic guard, also telegraphed to Monsignor McAlpine his sympathy and informed him that two aeroplanes were being despatched immediately from Baldonnell to search for any possible survivors.

Amongst other telegrams received was one from Mr. J.W. Mongan T.D., Carna who adjourned to Cleggan, where he joined the patrol boat the *Morochue* and went out to Inishbofin on Sunday evening to visit the homes of the bereaved people.

Mr. Mongan informed Fr. Diskin he would see that as far as it was in his power to relieve the suffering, he would do so and he believed that the government would also help.

Among other messages of sympathy, Fr O'Malley, Claddaghduff received the following telegram from the Archbishop of Tuam '*Deeply grieved at the awful tragedy, most sincere sympathy'.*

Relief Fund For The West

As promised by the President of Ireland, Mr. Liam T. Cosgrave, a worldwide appeal for help was made for the fishermen and their families on the 2nd of November 1927.

A year ago the world was shocked at the destruction by fire of some 50 of our people, in the village of Drumcollogher. The response to the appeal then made on behalf of the dependents of those who lost their lives in that fire was princely and enabled the committee to safeguard the future of those on whose behalf the fund was inaugurated. Today the power of the Almighty has again touched our people, and by a storm and flood has brought sorrow and desolation to the homes of some 40 of our hardy peasants who earn a precarious livelihood on our Western Coasts.

Living on the shores of the Atlantic, exposed to all the moods of the ocean, they wrung from the sea and from its rocky shores a bare existence. A God-fearing, thrifty, hardworking race, they were content with their lot and sought to bring up their children to face the dangers of the deep and the hardships of the daily round with the courage they inherited from generations of seafolk like themselves.

The storm which passed over our island on Friday, the 28th October, utterly wiped out the breadwinners of several villages, and destroyed their frail boats and fishing gear. The generous feelings of our people have been stirred to the depths. There is widespread anxiety to help those who are left and to do something which will help to prevent a recurrence of so appalling a calamity.

In response to what I know to be the wishes of our people I have decided to make a public appeal for funds to enable the committee which I have invited to act to relieve the immediate wants of those who have been deprived of their breadwinners and to ensure that so far as may be, the future well being of these poor people will be safeguarded. Should a surplus remain when these objects have been achieved, the committee should be empowered to prepare a scheme for the disposal of that surplus in such manner as shall seem to them best in the interests of the Western Fisherfolk.

In the name of the Nation, I appeal to the Nation to subscribe to the fund which is being opened for the relief of those who have suffered and for the other purposes mentioned above. I do so with confidence, knowing that I am but the mouthpiece of our people and am but voicing their desire to bring succour to those whom the hand of the Lord hath touched.

Until this appeal went to press, a sum of £12,000 had been subscribed for the relief of the relatives of the fishermen who had lost their lives. This money had been collected in two weeks, and by the time the President's appeal closed in February 1928, a total of £36,719 (equivalent to more than £1.6 million in today's terms) had been collected from sources all over Ireland and beyond.

At the time, it was recorded that, with the exception of a disaster in which a picture house had been destroyed in Drumcollogher (Co Limerick), no tragedy had aroused so much popular sympathy.

In President Cosgrave's timely appeal for aid, it was stated that after the immediate needs of the stricken communities had been covered, the committee formed to control the funds would devise a scheme for disposal of the remaining funds in a manner that would reflect the best interests of the fishermen's families.

The disaster revealed the full extent of the poverty experienced by the western fishermen and their dependants. It became clear that the people of western fishing communities lived not as independent citizens in a free land, but as slaves in intolerable conditions

The Gaeltacht Commission had made at least a constructive effort to redeem these appalling conditions. The revelations of such poverty touched the hearts of people everywhere, who responded with enormous generosity. The storm that had swept away lives, also swept away the smugness of those who appeared to believe that people who had survived famine and penal laws would be content to survive in conditions of callous neglect at the hands of their fellow countrymen.

Conditions were so bad that, within a week of the disaster, the communities felt compelled to adopt a new plan of action for their own preservation. A meeting was held, at which it was decided to form local committees in each district. The committees would consist of the parish priest and other suitable individuals, and would be responsible for determining and dealing with the needs of the people affected. Funds would be at their disposal for the immediate relief of the victims' families. A standing sub-committee was appointed, at the same time, to dispose of urgent matters and to look after general administration details arising between meetings of the national committee. In the first year, five meetings of the national committee took place along with nine meetings of the sub-committee.

COMMITTEES SET UP
First meeting of the National Relief Fund Committee

The national committee consisted of the following people: President Cosgrave; the Most Reverend T.P. Gilmartin, DD, Archbishop of Tuam; the Most Reverend James Naughton, DD, Bishop of Killala; the Rt. Reverend Monsignor McAlpine, PP, VG; the Very Reverend M. Quinn, PP; the Very Reverend A.M. Dodd, PP; the Reverend John Diskin; Sir John Lumsden, KBE, MD; Professor E.P. Culverwell, MA, FTCD; Dr W. Lombard Murphy; Sir Joseph A. Glynn; Messrs A.A. Hall, L.C. Moriarty, George Crosbie, Patrick Crowley, T.C. McDonagh, H.G. Connolly and John Healy. The first meeting of the committee was held on November 12th, 1927.

It was decided that a comprehensive scheme to relieve the distress occasioned by the fishing disaster off the coasts of Galway and Mayo would be prepared by the committee. In view of the difficulty of obtaining the attendance of all the members of the committee, it was decided that those members living in Dublin should form a sub-committee, with power to deal with matters of detail in the intervals between meetings of the full National Committee.

The Committee understood that a number of local entertainments (concerts, dances, etc.) were being organised in aid of the Fund, and they asked that the organisers of such events should communicate immediately with the Honorary Secretary to the Committee, so that formal authorisation from the National Committee could be issued. It is considered that such authority would be in the interests of the promoters of *bona fide* entertainments and of the fund.

The Archbishop of Tuam handed in a cheque for £532, being the subscriptions personally received by His Grace. Monsignor MacAlpine presented a cheque for £816, the sum received by him to date.

A number of suggestions for ameliorating the condition of those suffering as a result of the disaster were discussed by the Committee, and were referred to the sub-committee for further consideration.

Sir John Lumsden mentioned that he had been asked if it would be possible for bodies of workers in factories, etc., to combine together to buy fishing boats to replace those lost, the idea being that each boat so purchased would be associated with the particular sets of workers contributing.

Western Fishing Disaster Fund meeting

On the 26th of November 1927 a meeting was held of the local committee of the Western Fishing Disaster Dependents Fund.

At this meeting Monsignor McAlpine again emphasised the necessity for pressure to be brought to bear on the government, in the hope that some active steps would be taken in connection with the apportionment of lands in the immediate vicinity of the affected area of Rossadilisk. He stated that, if these poor families were not taken out of their present wretched surroundings, they would remain in perpetual poverty. He had being greatly moved and appalled by the scandalous conditions in which these people lived.

Dr. Lavelle (Letterfrack) suggested that the shell fishing industry in Connemara should be developed on proper lines. He pointed out that there was a colossal business in France and the United States. The French oyster beds, he added, were actually planted from Connemara beds. He commented on the fact that the splendid oyster bed in Ballinakill Bay was neglected. Dr. Lavelle also expressed the opinion that the rug making and carpet weaving industry should be established, as these industries did not require a lot of capital.

It was proposed to write to the Ministry of Fisheries asking them to send a representative to examine the conditions on the spot and confer with the local committee as to what might be done.

Galway County Council Finance Committee meeting

The Finance Committee of Galway County Council met on Saturday the 10th of December 1927. At this meeting Mr. Michael McNeill passed the following resolution 'that the government be called on to take over the available grass lands in Rossadilisk for division among the landless fishermen immediately'.

Following this statement a letter was read from Mr. L.A. Moriarty, the secretary of the Minister of Fisheries. On the subject of the provision of suitable fishing boats for the fishermen on the West Coast, it went as follows:

I am directed by the Minister of Fisheries to state that the department is at all times ready to consider applications from fishermen for loans to purchase the class of fishing boats which the applicants consider suitable for their requirements. The Minister's attention has been called to the suggestions appearing in the public press and elsewhere, that the small inshore fishermen should be provided with large boats in which to follow their calling with greater security. Large boats can not be kept in safety at most of the centres on our west coast, where the fishermen and farmers are most numerous. Even where good, natural harbours do exist, the larger boat is not as portable to the fishermen, as the handy yawl, or even canoe. A large boat requires expensive repairs from time to time, as when used intermittently only it deteriorates more rapidly than would be the case if kept at work constantly. Again such a large boat will be a remunerative investment only when fishing for mackerel and herrings, for the catching of which it is specially designed.

INISHBOFIN AND ROSSADILISK DEVELOPMENT
Fishing

The local demand by the fishermen and their spokesmen was for larger boats in which to follow herring and other types of fish. In 1924 and 1925, the Department had run a trial in Cleggan, manning one large motor boat with a crew from Rossadilisk and Inishbofin. The purpose was to see whether a large boat would be cost effective, but the results were disappointing.

When the Disaster Committee urged the Department to provide the survivors of the Cleggan Bay disaster with larger boats, in order to avoid further similar tragedies, it was pointed out that such a course of action would be inadvisable without further trials.

The Department accordingly decided to run another, larger trial, and in the summer of 1928, six large motor vessels equipped for herring fishing were sent to Cleggan. The crews of these boats were comprised of expert Donegal fishermen, accustomed to offshore herring fishing, along with local men from Inishbofin and Rossadilisk, who would be trained in that method of fishing. Their objective was to explore the waters between Slyne Head and Achill Head for herring, and to train the local crews before any commitment was made to supply the crews with expensive boats.

The trial was unsuccessful in locating herring in the region and the Department concluded that a herring fishery was not viable. Instead, it was decided that the men could be profitably employed in lobster fishing with the aid of smaller motorised vessels that could also be used for line fishing, trawling and seining. A boat of this type was sent to Cleggan in the summer of 1929.

The results of fishing with this boat were very poor, with only twelve pounds being made in four weeks. Consequently, the Department was unable to recommend that the West Coast Disaster Committee should use its funds to provide motorised fishing boats to the fishermen of the Cleggan district. Instead, it was considered that fishing in canoes and row boats, when the weather permitted, would be the most profitable industry for these men.

Improved service with islands

The Disaster Committee approved a grant of five hundred pounds in order to provide a more suitable boat to ply between the islands in the Cleggan area. It was decided by the Committee that a medium-sized motor boat, capable of carrying passengers, mail and livestock, would be best suited to providing a daily service between Cleggan and the islands of Inishbofin and Inishark. A contract to build such a boat was placed in 1931 and a loan system was granted by the Department of Fisheries to the prospective owner, who would be guaranteed three mail runs per week.

Cottage industries

Consideration was given to setting up various cottage industries in the area, but difficulties arose in establishing such projects. Although the Department purchased ten knitting machines, with the intention of employing twelve workers from Rossadilisk and Claddaghduff. Investigation revealed no memory of where the machines were placed or whether the scheme ever actually generated any employment in these two communities.

Actions taken with lands

After much discussion and numerous letters being sent back and forth over the years, the lands in Cleggan and the surrounding areas were divided up among the people, to try and improve their situation. The entire process took about three years.

The Feeneys, one of the Murray families and the O'Tooles were moved to parts of the estate of Charles B. Freyer (Major Dermot

Freyer). Other families were also moved to areas around the district, whilst some stayed in Rossadilisk, where more land was given to them. This was all discussed with the people themselves and with the land commission, with whose consent an agreement was reached.

Another fishing disaster

Within a few months of the inauguration of the fund, a second but fortunately smaller, disaster occurred in the vicinity of the Aran Islands. Two fishermen were drowned on this occasion, leaving thirteen dependants. It was decided by the national committee to extend the benefits of the fund to these dependents also.

What happened regarding funds

On the 14th of December 1927 Mr. John Healy, Honorary Secretary of the National Committee visited the areas affected and he submitted the following report (some details have been omitted regarding some of the families mentioned).

On the afternoon of the 30th of November 1927, I went to Galway and next proceeded to Clifden accompanied by Mr. Thomas McDonagh, a member of the committee. At Clifden we met the Right Reverend Monsignor McAlpine, P.P. and with him went to the village of Rossadilisk taking up his curate Father O'Malley on the way.

This village suffered severely, sixteen of its men folk being victims. Five of these were married and the widows survive as well as twenty-eight children under 17 years of age. The unmarried men left dependants comprising two fathers, four mothers, and three dependent brothers and sister, a total in all of forty-two dependants.

The families of many of the victims were visited. The weather was wet and stormy, and the sorrow of the bereaved ones and the wretched housing conditions all combined to make the scene a truly pitiable one.

A committee of residents in Clifden and Cleggan is in charge of the arrangements for the distribution of relief and it was learned that grants amounting to £20 were made to each family. This aid took the form of orders on local shopkeepers to provide value in kind to the sum named. The grants appear to have been arrived at in a somewhat haphazard fashion and each family was placed on the same level irrespective of the extent of the loss incurred, the number of dependants, etc.

Mr. McDonagh and I gathered that there were some differences of opinion amongst the committee as to the best method of meeting the requirements. This was only to be expected seeing that it consists of thirty members. Looking at the position generally and in view of the fact that arrangements had been made for the time being to meet the distress, we thought that any detailed discussion on our part might to advantage be deferred.

Before leaving Clifden the following morning we had an opportunity of seeing Mr. Lavelle, the Joint Honorary Secretary (with Fr. O'Malley) to the committee, and it was arranged that he would forward the minutes of the meeting, allowances sanctioned and other information regularly to the general committee in Dublin. The meetings are held every Saturday.

Inishbofin

Another afflicted centre is Inishbofin: we were unable, owing to weather condition, to cross over to the island. The wants of the sufferers here are also being looked after by the Clifden and Cleggan committee, above referred to, and the administrator of the island, Father Diskin, is a member of it. The remarks as to distribution, etc already made in the case of Rossadilisk, also apply here. The victims from the island numbered nine. Of these two were married, the widows survive and thirteen children under 17 years of age. Other dependants are 3 fathers, 4 mothers, 4 brothers and sisters under 14 years of age, and an invalid brother aged 20 making it a total of twenty-seven.

It need hardly be observed that the degree of loss varies in almost every case both here and at Rossadilisk. Many circumstances require to be taken into consideration and much discrimination will require to be used in arriving at a fair and reasonable allowance to each family. The rough and ready method adopted by the local committee already referred to should be discouraged.

The areas of Rossadilisk and Inishbofin lie within the Archdiocese of Tuam. The remaining two areas whose people suffered from the disaster are Inniskea Islands North and South, off Mayo, and Lacken on the mainland. Father Dodd in whose parish the two Islands are included lives a few miles from Belmullet. We called upon him on the 3rd of December. The number of victims is ten. One was married and leaves a widow and seven children, the youngest only two months old. The dependants are five fathers, six mothers, ten brothers, seven sisters and one invalid brother, a total of thirty-seven dependants.

Father Dodd had a complete knowledge of the conditions of each family. He had no committee but was helped by a reliable parishioner from one of the islands. Up to the present, Father Dodd has been able from funds in hand to meet the requirements. After some discussion as to the best way to deal with the cases in his area, he gave us much encouragement by all the businesslike manner in which he met suggestions. He fully shared the views put before him as to the necessity for providing only for the reasonable wants of the poor people and that no extravagance in the allowances should be permitted.

We then went fully with him into each case, the loss incurred and the circumstances of the several families, and without much difficulty we were able to agree on a tentative scheme of weekly payments.

Father Dodd asked that a bonus might be given to the men who helped recover and bury the victims. I asked Father Dodd to suggest a reasonable sum.

Lacken

We visited Father Quinn, who resides a short distance from the scene of the disaster off Lacken. The number of victims in this area is nine. Two were married, and in each case a widow was left. In the second case, there are two children. In this area also two families were each deprived of two sons. The other dependants are, three fathers, three mothers, one brother 11 years old, and four sisters 17 years of age and under, in all fifteen dependants. The circumstances in connection with the management of the cases are similar to the case at Inniskea.

Father Quinn had complete knowledge of the facts. He, like Fr. Dodd, was in agreement with us as to the manner in which assistance should, at least tentatively, be given. After some discussion we agreed on an allowance, meanwhile Fr. Quinn has sufficient funds in hand to supply the wants of the dependants.

We next called on his Grace the Most Reverend Doctor Gilmartin, Archbishop of Tuam, and had a discussion generally on the situation. His Grace was particularly anxious that the committee should consider the desirability of dividing the fund, assigning one portion for the benefit of the dependants in the affected areas within the Archdiocese (this would embrace Rossadilisk and Boffin), and the other portion for the benefit of those within the Diocese of Killala, which includes the Inniskea Islands and Lacken.

His Grace pointed out that machinery already existed in the Archdiocese for applying in a methodical manner of trust and other funds for specific purpose and he thought no difficulty would arise in dispensing satisfactorily and in accordance with previously arranged regulations any money placed in the hands of the Diocesan Authorities.

The Bishop of Killala (Most Reverend James Naughton) did not, at our interview make any similar suggestion in regard to the cases in his Lordship's diocese.

I did not deal with the aspect bearing on the re-instatement of boats, nets, gear, etc. lost as the subcommittee invited the Department of Fisheries, through Mr. Moriarty, to undertake that branch of the work, and although the subject was mentioned by Fathers Dodd and Quinn we thought it best to avoid discussion and leave the question in the hands of the Department.

Following submission of this report, another review of the conditions was recorded on the 10th January 1928. There was a lot of business to be dealt with regarding bills outstanding and the procedures that needed to be put in place before any progress could be made with the local committees and the National Committee: in the meantime, these poor people were no better off.

Report 10th January 1928

As desired by the sub-committee, I went to Clifden and by prior arrangement Mr. McDonagh and I met a member of the local committee. Monsignor McAlpine was present but Father Diskin and Father O'Malley, in direct charge of the Boffin and Rossadilisk areas respectively, were unable to attend, as it was the eve of a holiday.

I explained the object of my visit, to see the families of the victims of the disaster and obtain information to enable tentative payments to the dependants to be fixed. It was difficult to reconcile the members of the committee to the decision that no further allocations should be made without the sanction of the General Committee impressed upon them the fact that the Committee intended to exercise full control over all distribution and that it would consequently be necessary for the local Committee to examine carefully all bills for supplies before submitting them for payment so as to secure that no unreasonable or excessive items were charged .A general discussion ensued in which attempts were made to justify the two allocations already made in each case. Eventually it was agreed that a sub-committee should meet Mr. McDonagh and myself on the following day to see what, if any, accounts could be immediately dealt with. At Friday's meeting the whole of the members again attended, Father O'Malley being also present. Some of the members again pressed for a further allocation to each family but as an arrangement for direct tentative payments would soon be settled the matter was not pressed.

A discussion also took place on the question of the payment of debts to shopkeeper's etc, incurred anterior to the disaster by the families of the victims. The members were almost unanimously in favour of the proposal but Monsignor McAlpine opposed Mr. McDonagh and I pointed out that we could only express our personal opinion which was in agreement with that of Monsignor McAlpine. As many of the debts claimed for were in excess of the returns made to the General Committee it was arranged that Fr. Diskin and Fr. O'Malley should make further enquiry into the project and report. It was made clear however to the meeting that the collection was in no way committing the General Committee to payment of the debts. The question of payment of the allocation of twenty pounds made to each family for the goods supplied and also for the outlay in connection with the supply of coffins, interments etc, was discussed but as only partial accounts and when examined and vouched for to forward them to the General Committee.

The weather conditions being unfavourable to cross over to Boffin it was agreed that Monsignor McAlpine and Fr. Diskin and Fr. O'Malley should make enquiries into the various cases and suggest tentative payments, the list of these suggested payments to be sent forward for the consideration and approval of the General Committee.

Another important matter was discussed, that of preparing and forwarding a statement of what local industries could with advantage he established to enable the people in the district to secure more employment. The local committee agreed to enquire into the question and forward the views of its members as soon as possible.

Although, owing to unfavourable weather, we did not attain the immediate object of our visit was the arranging of a scheme of tentative payments, we had the satisfaction of placing clearly before the local committee the views held by the general committee in regard to indiscriminate allocations, etc, and we believe that much good will result from our personal interviews with the members of the local committee.

I brought back the cheque which was given me to pay commitments of the local committee if some were approved but as stated above the accounts had not been fully dealt with.

The following shows the total number of victims and dependents in each of the areas affected

Areas	Victims	Dependents	
Rossadilisk	16		60
Inishbofin	9		37
Lacken	9		27
Inniskea	10		50
Aran	2		13

New boats and gear supplied by February 1929 as reported

Local committees were set up in each district and entrusted with funds to relieve the immediate wants of the dependants of the victims.

In addition to looking after the needs of these 187 persons, the sub-committee also undertook to ascertain, through the local clergy, the losses of boats, nets, and gear in the various areas. Prompt arrangements were made with the Department of Fisheries for the immediate supply of new boats, nets and gear required. In the first year, 15 fully equipped boats were supplied to the immediate dependants of the victims, and nine boats and equipment to other fishermen who lost their boats on the night of the October storm. In addition, boats were repaired and large quantities of nets and special gear supplied to fishermen who suffered losses from the effects of the storm.

Suggested principles for assistance

The following suggestions were put forward for consideration by the committee when deciding the basis upon which relief would be distributed to the dependants:

1. Pensions for life to:- Widows, sisters and brothers, if delicate, and one sister entirely dependent on drowned brother.
2. Pensions to fathers and mothers up to 70 years of age if not already in receipt of old age pensions.
3. Children's allowances to widows or parents of the victims on the following basis:- 5/- a week for each son and daughter between 10 and 20 years, 2/6d a week for each child under 10 years, 5/- a week for each sister of a victim between 10 and 20 years.

If these principles were applied, the number to receive benefit would be reduced to 143:

Widows: 10 pensions for life or to the age of 70 years.

Parents: 23 pensions up to 70 years

Delicate brother and sisters: 12 pensions up to 70 years

Delicate sisters: 1 pension up to 70 years

Children of victims: 55 to receive an allowance

Young brother and sisters: 36 to receive an allowance

Other dependent relatives: 6 to receive allowance and pensions

This method of relieving the day-to-day needs of the dependants with weekly payments was purely tentative. After careful consideration, the national committee decided that it would be more advantageous to allocate £100 to each of the families, in order to enable them to pay their debts at once.

Deed of trust drawn up

A deed of trust was also drawn up under which the following were appointed trustees of the fund: President Cosgrave, Dr. W. Lombard Murphy, Sir Joseph A. Glynn and Mr. A.A. Hall. The deed provided, amongst other things for:

1. The extension of the Lady Dudley nursing scheme to the fishing villages or districts of the western coast affected by the disaster, which, in the opinion of the National Committee were not adequately supplied with nursing facilities.
2. Improvement in the supply and maintenance of transport and communication by motor boats or otherwise between islands and the mainland.
3. The relief of any future need or distress, which may arise by reason

of storm, flood, famine, disease or other misfortune of a public
nature, amongst the fisherfolk of the western coast and islands.

4. Such other charitable purposes for the benefit of the fisherfolk
   generally of the western coast and islands as the National
   Committee should from time to time think proper.

The National Committee also had the power to set aside money or
investment as a special fund to provide for any of the purposes
authorised in the Deed of Trust provisions. It was reported at the
time that the National Committee made investments in approved
securities, the interest from which would be applied to meet the
various objects of the trust.

Dissatisfaction shown by the dependants of victims

As the following letters make clear, the dispersal of funds and the actual
relief received by the victims' dependants caused great dissatisfaction
in the communities involved. In spite of the huge response to the appeal
for funds, their hardship continued. The letters were sent to John Healy,
the Secretary of the West Coast Disaster National Relief Fund.

Dear Sir,

*I enclose a letter which speaks for itself. Murrey is one of the
crew that came safe last October, the night of the disaster, and he
payed a gale that was due at the time although he had his net last.*

*We understood here that all the arrears of the nets lost were to
be wiped off and now Murrey only asked time until July and he is
told he must pay at once.*

*Murrey has only a canoe that's over 20 years old and is
entirely unseaworthy and has only a boy of 15 years to fish with
and to fish at all has to leave the canoe anchored because its too
heavy to be carried on the bank. Now Murrey lost his way of
living through the disaster and because he came safe surely that's
not the reason that himself and his family should be let starve. He
asked for a new canoe but would not get it unless on loan and I
am very doubtful if he could get suretys for to get it on loan.*

*I will be very grateful if you look into this case and see if
anything can be done.*

Yours truly,

John J. Coyne

Innisboffin,
Cleggan, P. O.
Co. Galway.
22th Jan. 1930.

Sir,
There's great dissatisfaction amongst us regarding the distribution of the "West Coast Fishing Disaster Fund". I think that money is not utilized for the purpose for which it was collected. During the past two years we have not been dealt with adequately, and have not been allocated sufficient money for our support. etc.

Therefore, we (the undersigned dependants of Innisboffin, Inniskea, & Rossadilisk) now demand a general distribution of that enormous fund to be made on or ~~be~~ before February 7th 1930.

We Remain. Sir.
Yours Truly:—

Owen McGinty
William Reilly
Thomas Meenaghan.
Patrick Keane
John Monaghan
Mrs John Meenaghan

Inniskea South,
Belmullet,.
Co Mayo.

Mrs Michael Reilly ⎤ Inniskea North.
Mrs Michael Lavelle ⎦ Belmullet. Co Mayo.

James Tierney
Catherine O'Toole
May Connelly
Mary Scuffle.
Catherine McHale
John Concannon
Anne King.
⎫
⎬ Innis Boffin
⎭ East end
    Co Galway.

Anthony Davis ⎤ Aughrismore
Kate Delap ⎦ Claddaghduff, Co. Galway.
Martin Laffey
Michael Feeney
Mrs Margaret Cloonan
Mrs Lacey
Mrs Jane Murray,
Mrs. Bridget O'Toole
Mrs Mary Lacey (Mark
Mrs. Bridget Murry
Margaret Feeney
E. Halloran .
⎫
⎬ Rossadilisk,
⎭ Cleggan Claddaghduff,
    Co Galway.

After receipt of these letters, the following report was prepared by the Secretary:

Distribution of West Coast Fund

The letter of the 22nd of January last signed by the dependents and others of the victims of the disaster, resident in three of the four areas affected, expressing dissatisfaction with the manner in which the fund is being distributed and demanding a general distribution to be made before the 7th of February, 1930, is submitted for consideration.

The letter is addressed from Inishbofin, Cleggan Post Office, Co. Galway and the areas represented are Inishbofin, Rossadilisk, and Inniskea, Co. Mayo. That of Rathlacken is omitted. The names appended to the letter correctly represented the parties in each of the three mentioned areas who are in receipt of relief from the fund and it will be observed that many of the signatures are in the same handwriting.

The attention of the committee was called some time ago to the publication of letters in the Irish Independent *of the 19th April, 1929, and 22nd August, 1929, casting reflections on the administration of the fund and incidentally helping to create discontent amongst the fishermen regarding the administration of the fund. The first of these letters was signed 'Cleggan' and it is suggested that it is more than a coincidence that the letter of the 22nd of January, now under consideration, is addressed from the neighbourhood of Cleggan and shows, I think, that it was composed by someone in a higher station of life than fishermen. The letter 'Cleggan' published in the* Irish Independent *of 19th April was prepared by and inserted in the paper at the request of a Catholic clergyman. The letter signed by 'West Coast Fishermen' which appeared in the issue of the same paper of 22nd August last, reflecting on the treatment meted out to the dependants living on Inniskea Island by the National Committee was likewise the emanation of a clergyman. The statements in this letter were so serious that it was necessary to take steps to refute them. Hence the publication of letters of 31st August following from the Parish Priest of the Islands, Fr. Dodd which showed that many of the statements were exaggerated and others untrue. The invitation in this correspondence extended to 'West Coast Fishermen' to disclose their identity in view of the very distinct contradiction of his statements by Fr. Dodd was not of course accepted.*

It is known that the writer is not attached to either of the dioceses in which the Inniskea Islands and West Cork are respectively situated, but the gentlemen spent a holiday on the Islands of Inniskea shortly before his letter of 22nd August appeared. Another attack, somewhat similar to this mentioned above, was made on the National Committee by the finance committee of the Galway County Council at a meeting held in September last. It is a curious fact that the letter from these dependants now under consideration, that of 'Cleggan' and the attack by the finance committee of the Galway County Council are associated with the districts of Rossadilisk and Inishbofin and points to the probability that these various attacks were instigated by one individual who might be found on inquiry to be 'West Cork Fishermen'.

In connection with the attempts to have the whole of the fund that was collected at once distributed among the dependants and relatives of those who lost their lives, it is useful to refer to the National Appeal that was made shortly after the disaster.

It stated that the appeal for funds was made to enable the committee to relieve the immediate wants of those who have been deprived of their breadwinners and to ensure that so far as may be the future well being of these poor people will be safeguarded. Should a surplus remain when these objects have been achieved the committee should be empowered to prepare a scheme for the disposal of that surplus in such manner as shall seem to them best in the interests of the Western fisherfolk.

It is not usual as a general rule to take serious notice of anonymous correspondents in newspapers but when as in this case the administration of a large fund subscribed to by a benevolent public from all parts of the world is attacked and where it can be shown that some at least of the attacks are made by responsible people, it is not only justifiable but almost essential that the administrators should take all possible steps to vindicate their position. Especially it is necessary in this particular instance in as much as that some of the statements made in the letters published in the Independent *were copied as news and transmitted to the Editors of newspapers in Great Britain and America for publication thus helping to create a certain amount of suspicion in the minds of subscribers to the fund as to the manner of its disposal.*

Further letters and abstracts from the Relief Fund accounts appear in the appendices at the end of this book.

It would appear that the development of the communities after the disaster was affected by a degree of neglect and lack of planning by the committees, official agencies and government departments.

The conflicting feelings of the dependants about their conditions at the time were unfortunate and should have been avoided. It must be acknowledged, however, that the task of the National Relief Fund Committee, in trying to come to decisions that effected some 187 people, was not an easy one..

The size of the committees, along with the lack of representation from among the fishing communities themselves, raises questions as to the efficacy of making decisions which would be in the best interest of the communities and their future. Clear policy guidelines on the future development of the marine environment, with better structures in place, would have been of long term benefit to all who had been affected by the disaster.

The communities of Rossadilisk, Inishbofin, Inniskea and Lacken never fully recovered. Even today, the ruined gables of the cottages stand out starkly against the sky as a natural monument to the disaster of 1927.

Above: *An aerial view of Inishbofin.*
Below: *Transport between the islands and the mainland*

Present day views of Inishbofin taken by John Abeyta.

Inishbofin circa 1960s. (Photographs courtesy of Inishbofin Development Association Committee)

Disaster survivor, Festy Feeney, with his wife Nora.
(Photograph by Michael Feeney)

EPILOGUE

IN 1956 MY GRANDFATHER, Festy Feeney, was a lonely fisherman, as he recalled all his memories of the disaster. When he put out his curragh from Rossadilisk, he usually had the sea to himself, except for the shadows of a stalwart race of fishermen who once braved the waters of the rugged Connemara coast with cheerful strength. At that time, when Michael O'Halloran interviewed him, he was an old man of 73 years, and a curragh weighed heavily on top of his old shoulders. His story, like that of many others who were left behind, is a reminder to us today that these people suffered a loss that can only be imagined. We, as a community, should be very proud of those who lost their lives striving to provide a better life for their families.

Much was taken from these people on October 28th 1927. The relatives of the victims were left without any means of survival. Many people left the villages, some to go as far as America. As a result of the storm, Rossadilisk, in particular, became virtually uninhabited. The few families that remained barely scraped by on the relief and were grateful for the emotional support of friends and relatives. Rossadilisk changed from being a lively fishing village to a virtual ghost town and the scars can still be seen there today.

The effects that a storm, a natural phenomenon, has had on these communities is still evident some 74 years on: just ruins of old homes that belonged to loving, happy families all pulling together to make a living. To an onlooker on a sunny day, the glorious beaches and inviting blue waters give little indication of the destruction and devastation caused in peoples' lives by a brutal storm. The memory, however, lives on in the hearts of those left behind, many of whom are now scattered far and wide as a result of that appalling night. Whatever mistakes may have been made by those responsible for providing relief to the victims, the fact remains that, wherever people make a living from the sea, the possibility of natural disaster wreaking havoc in their lives is an ever present reality.

Thankfully, those who go to sea today have a better chance of survival due to the wonderful work of the RNLI and the Air/Sea Rescue teams. Men and women from the local communities risk their own lives as members of lifeboat crews, ready to brave rough seas and heavy gales in order to help their comrades in peril on the ocean.

MICHAEL O TOOLE	1927	MARTIN LACEY	1949	JAMES KENNY	1800s	BRIDGET KERRIGAN	1900
THOMAS SCUFFLE	1927	MICHAEL LACEY	1949	MICHAEL CUNNANE	1800s	JOHN TIERNEY	1908
PATRICK KING	1927	PETER LACEY	1949	JOHN HUGHES	1800s	JAMES NAUGHTON	1908
JOHN LAVELL	1927	JOHN COMEY		TIM PAT O'TOOLE	1800s	CONSTABLE McCARTHY	1908
PAT POWELL	1927	LAWRENCE CANNON		PRICE	1800s	ALAN LYDON	1908
JOHN CONNOLLY	1927	JOHN LACEY		REILLY	1800s	JAMES CALLAGHAN	1908
HARRY LAVELLE	1927	MARTIN BAKER		CUNNANE	1800s	MICHAEL EARLY	1908
MICHAEL TIERNEY	1927	ANTHONY DIAMOND		BARRETT	1800s	PADRAIG LACEY	1909
MARTIN MCHALE	1927	JOYCE		WALSH	1800s	CLOONAN	1909
MICK CLOHERTY	1942	PHILIP KERRIGAN		PETER BARRETT	1800s	CUSHIN	1900 s
JOHN SCUFFLE	1942	PATRICK PRENDERGAST		PATRICK TIERNEY	1800s	MICHAEL NAUGHTON	1900 s
JOE TIERNEY	1942	GEORGE LACEY		O'HALLORAN BROTHERS	1800s	REDMOND DAVIS	1914
COLMAN KING	1942	PATRICK LACEY		FESTY McCANN	1885	PATRICK CLOONAN	1914
ROBERT JOHNSTON	1959	GEORGE LACEY		PATRICK McCANN	1885	GEORGE LACEY	1914
RICHARD MATHES	1976	PATRICK MORAN		JOHN KERRIGAN	1900	TOM WALLACE	1914
EDWARD MOLL	1976	BRIAN LAVELLE		MICHAEL BARRETT	1900	TOM BAKER	1914
JOHN LAVELLE	1976	PAT LAVELLE				PATRICK PRENDERGAST	1920 s
JOHNNY CUNNANE	1994	PETER SCHOFIELD					
LAWRANCE WARD	1995	PETER NAUGHTON					
PAMELA O HALLORAN	1995						

Inishbofin memorial by John Behan. (photographed by Marie Coyne)

THE DISASTER SONG
by Patrick Tierney

All loyal people throughout the nation
combine with me and lend an ear
to this doleful tragedy I am revealing
that has caused many a silent tear.

This sad disaster, nothing came faster
being in October, we long mind the date
when those brave fishermen went out fishing
on Friday night, the twenty-eighth.

They left their homes late in the evening
about five o'clock as I now relate
but little thinking, as the stars were blinking
that they would meet with a drowning fate.

When a violent hurricane bore down upon them
where large vessels would have shrieking shrouds
it was a dead tornado of cyclone nature
that scattered rainbows and burst the clouds.

With lightning flashing and thunder rolling
men could not see where they could go.
Some tried in vain their homes to gain
against pouring rain being mixed with snow.

It caused a great sensation along every station
while brave men were fighting against splash and spray
which leaves bones steeping and many weeping
from Rossadilisk to Lacken Bay.

When the tempest gathered around Bofin Island
it caused great excitement all night till day
fearing our best and fondest would be borne from us
it was just the same in Inniskea.

Many left their homes in search of the tidings
as they walked along with light in hand
I could see fond mothers and widows wailing
as they knelt in prayer on the barren sand.

To see the children in deep distraction
they wrung their hands and their hair they tore
crying "Dear fathers and loving brothers
are we to part for evermore?".

Like bells when tolling, high seas were rolling
then one boat came safe to a Bofin strand
told how they spent the night between death and life
but now thanking God they were safe on land.

With hardships enduring while on their mooring
with a crew of four there were praises due
when the sea near filled her and swept their bailer
they bailed all night with a leather shoe.

When high winds were squalling they heard voices calling
but could not assist them nor yet reply
after this hearing they saw them disappearing
it was then they knew it was their drowning cry.

Next day to our surprise as the sun did rise
two boats came home from the mainland
and when they beached them, all rushed to meet them
with a fond greeting and a shake of hands.

O Virgin Mother, my heart does shudder
and our sad tale told to the world around
of our small fleet, most from one street
three boats came safe, whilst two were drowned.

If we could realise their thoughts when drowning
it was of the loved ones they left at home
for their upkeep out on the deep
where the crayfish creep, they met their doom.

I am overpowered with grief without relief
for the loss of dear friends that are now gone.
It is my intention no names to mention
I have this same feeling for every one.

With great sympathy to the Rossadilisk people
they were my friends when I crossed the bay
some of them were my relations that I will
see no more on Cleggan quay.

If they had employment from those that ruled them
that are up in Dublin they call the Dail
they would be at home with those that loved them
and not be drowned by a sudden squall.

So all befriended as my song's near ended
when on your knees I hope you will pray
to the God of Glory and Blessed Virgin
to save their souls on Judgement Day.

Gathering seaweed the traditional way at the East End of Inishbofin.
(Photograph by Frank McMullan A.F.A.I.P.)

Abstract of Receipts & Payments

RECEIPTS.

To Subscriptions received by Trustees				36,332	16	0
" Dividends on Investments:						
5% Compensation Stock to 1/5/1928	127	7	8			
5% War Loan Stock to 1/6/1928	150	0	0			
				277	7	8
" Bank Interest on credit balances				43	0	4

APPENDIX 1: *This page and the five following are abstracts from the accounts of the West Coast Disaster National Relief Fund, prepared by Kean and Company, Chartered Accountants, Dublin, for the period from 11th November, 1927 to 30th June 1928.*

PAYMENTS.

1928.
June 30 By Grants to Dependents.   4882   15   2

" Travelling Expenses.   68   10   0

" Printing & Stationery.   16   5   1

" Postage & Telegrams.   9   13   1

" Sundries.   2   16   9
                                                                    4980   0   1

" Balance in favour of the Fund –
   allocated as follows:–

   Transferred to Trustees of Dependents' Fund:

     Investments at cost:–

       £4000 5% War Loan Stk.   4080. 5. 4
       £1433.6.8 Bank of
         Ireland Stock.   4015.13.2
       £4,334 4½% Land Bonds   4058. 9.4
       £4,200 5% Dublin
         Corporation Stock.   3990. 0.0
       £4,050 5% Compensation
         Stock.   4036.19.4
                                            20,181   7   2

   Transferred to Trustees of Surplus
   Fund.

     Investments at Cost:–

       £2000 5% War Loan Stk.   2040. 2. 8
       £716.13.4 Bank of
         Ireland Stock.   2007.16. 7
       £2,166 4½% Land Bonds   2029. 4. 8
       £2,100 5% Dublin
         Corporation Stock.   1995. 0. 0
       £2,050 5% Compensation
         Stock.   2043. 8. 0
                                 10,115.11.11

     Cash in National
         Bank Ltd.   1,190. 8. 3
     Cash on hands.   185.16. 7   11,491   16   9
                                                                 31,673   3   11

                                                                 36,653   4   0

DR.

Abstract of Receipts & Payments

RECEIPTS.

1928.
June 30   To Balance in favour of the Fund

Investments at Cost:-

£4000 5% War Loan Stock.	4080	5	4			
£1433. 6. 8 Bank of Ireland Stock	4015	13	2			
£4334 4½% Land Bonds.	4058	9	4			
£4200 5% Dublin Corpn. Stock.	3990	0	0			
£4050 5% Compensation Stock.	4036	19	4			
				20,181	7	2

Dec. 31   " Dividends on Investments:-

5% War Loan Stock to 1/12/1928	100	0	0			
Bank of Ireland Stock to 30/6/1928	103	11	2			
4½% Land Bonds to 31/12/1928	165	15	0			
5% Dublin Corpn. Stock to 31/12/1928	178	10	0			
5% Compensation Stock to 1/11/1928	86	1	3			
				633	17	5
				20,815	4	7

ATIONAL (RELIEF) FUND.

FUND.
r ended   31st December, 1928.   CR.

PAYMENTS.

1928.
Dec. 31   By Grants to Dependents   1414   5 10

           " Balance in favour of the Fund –

               Investments at Cost:–

                   £4,000 5% War Loan Stock.   4080   5   4
                   £1,433.6. 8 Bank of Ireland Stock   4015   13   2
                   £4,334 4½% Land Bonds.   4058   9   4
                   £4,200 5% Dublin Corpn. Stock.   3990   0   0
                   £4,050 5% Compensation Stock.   4036   19   4
                                                        ─────────────
                                                        20,181   7   2
                   Less:
                       Amount due to Surplus Fund   780   8   5
                                                                   19,400   18   9

                                                                   20,815   4   7

DR.   Abstract of Receipts & Payment

RECEIPTS.

1929.
June 30   To Balance in favour of the Fund

           Investments at Cost:-

           £2,000 5% War Loan Stock.   2040   2   8
           £716.13. 4 Bank of Ireland Sock   2007   16   7
           £2156 - 4½% Land Bonds.   2029   4   8
           £2100 5% Dublin Corpn. Stoc   1995   0   0
           £2050 5% Compensation Stocl   2043   8   0

                                               10115   11   11

           Cash in National Bank Ltd.   1190   8   3

           Cash on hands.   185   16   7
                                                                11,491

Dec. 31   " Subscriptions received by Trustees
                 during half year.   387

           " Dividends on Investments:-

           5% War Loan Stock to 1/12/1928   50   0   0
           Bank of Ireland Stock to 30/6/1928   51   15   7
           4½% Land Bonds to 31/12/1928.   82   17   6
           5% Dublin Corpn.Stock to 31/12/1928   89   5   0
           5% Compensation Stock to 1/11/1928   43   11   3
                                                                 317

           " Bank Interest on Credit balances.   123

           " Surplus on Redemption of £600 - 5%
                 Compensation Stock.   1

                                                               12,321

<u>31st December, 1928.</u>   CR.

                    PAYMENTS.

1928.
Dec. 31   By Travelling Expenses.   63   3   6

           " Clerical Assistance.   235   0   0

           " Postage & Telegrams.   1   5   0

           " Sundries.   2   2   6
                                                                       301   11   0

           " Balance in favour of the Fund —

              Investments at Cost:—

                 £2000 5% War Loan Stock.   2040   2   8
                 £716.13.4 Bank of Ireland Stock.   2007   16   7
                 £2166 4½% Land Bonds.   2029   4   8
                 £2100 5% Dublin Corpn. Stock.   1995   0   0
                 £1450 5% Compensation Stock   1445   6   8

                                                     9517   10   7

              Cash in National Bank Ltd. includ-
                ing £600 realised from redemption
                of 5% Compensation Stock.   1700   14   7

              Cash on hands.   21   9   4

              Amount due by Dependents' Fund.   780   8   5
                                                                     12,020   2   11

                                                                     12,321   13   11

KEAN & COMPANY.
CHARTERED ACCOUNTANTS
AND
PUBLIC AUDITORS.
J BUCKLEY A C A
TELEPHONE Nº 21116.

16 & 17, Dame Street,

Dublin, 18th Feb. *19 37.*

The Trustees,

West Coast National (Relief) Fund,

Government Buildings,

Dublin.

Gentlemen,

We beg to enclose the Account of the Dependents' Fund and the Account of the Surplus Fund as made up for the year ended 31st December, 1936.

DEPENDENTS' FUND.

The charges for the year were as follows:-

Grants to Dependents.	£1993.10. 0	
Bank Charges & Cheque Book.	1.17. 8	
Making a total of		£1,995. 7. 8

The Income was as follows:-

Dividends on Investments.	323. 4. 4	
Bank Interest on Current Account	3. 9. 9	
Refund of Income Tax.	197. 3. 6	
Profit on sale of £1560 $4\frac{1}{2}$% Land Bonds.	228.10. 0	
Totalling		752. 7. 7

Showing an excess of Payments over Receipts of   £1,243. 0. 1 by which the balance in favour of the Fund at the end of the year has been reduced to £8,948.13.11 as compared with £10,182.14. 0 at 31st December, 1935.

2.

SURPLUS FUND.

The charge for the year as detailed in
the Account came to £802.12. 1

The Income was as follows:-

Dividends on Investments.	£237.18. 3	
Bank Interest on Current A/c	4.11. 6	
Refund of Income Tax.	133. 8. 2	
Profit on sale of £950 4½% Land Bonds.	150. 2.11	
		526. 0.10

Showing an excess of Payments over Receipts of   276.11. 3

by which the balance in favour of the Fund at the end of the year has

been reduced to £7,237. 1.11 as compared with £7,513.13. 2 at 31st

December, 1935.

We are,

Yours faithfully,

Kean & Co

APPENDIX 2: *These two pages and the four following are the Statement of Accounts of the West Coast Disaster National Relief Fund, prepared by Kean and Company, Chartered Accountants, Dublin, for the year ending 31st December 1936. (Documents courtesy of the National Archives, Dublin)*

DR.   Abstract of Receipts & Payments

RECEIPTS.

1936.
Jan. 1   To Balance in favour of the Fund viz:

          Investments at cost:

              £843.7.3   Bank of Ireland Stock.   2,629   2   5
              £4073   4½% Land Bonds.   3,911   19   9
              £3600   5% Dublin Corpn. Stock.   3,420   0   0
                                                       9,961   2   2

          Cash in National Bank - as adjusted   221   11   10
                                                                        10,182

Dec. 31   " Dividends on Investments viz:

              Bank of Ireland Stock to 30/6/36   88   4   9
              Dublin Corpn.Stock to 31/12/36.   139   10   0
              4½% Land Bonds.   95   9   7
                                                                         323

          " Bank Interest on Credit Balance.   3

          " Refund of Income Tax.   197

          " Profit on sale of Investments viz:

              £1560   4½% Land Bonds.   228

                                                                       10,935

<pre>
                    31st December, 1936.   CR.

          PAYMENTS.

By Grants to Dependents.   1,993   10   0

 " Bank Charges & Cheque Book.   1   17   8

 " Balance in favour of the Fund viz:

     Investments at cost:

       £843.7.3 Bank of Ireland Stock.   2,629   2   5
       £2513   4½% Land Bonds.   2,413 13   6
       £3600   5% Dublin Corpn.Stock.   3,420   0   0
                                          8,462 15 11

     Cash in National Bank – as adjusted   287 11   6

     Income Tax Refund due   197   3   6
                                          ─────────────
                                          8,947 10 11

     Less:
         Dividend due to Purchaser of
         £450 4½% Land Bonds.   7 17   0
                                                          8,939 13 11

                                                         10,935   1   7
</pre>

DR.   Abstract of Receipts & Payments

RECEIPTS.

1936.
Jan. 1   To Balance in favour of the Fund viz:

          Investments at cost:

          £1085.5.8   Bank of Ireland Stock.   3,303 19   5
          £2266   4½% Land Bonds.   2,195 19 11
          £1800   5% Dublin Corpn. Stock.   1,710   0   0
                                                  7,209 19   4

          Cash in National Bank - as adjusted   312   1   7

          Cash on hand (Petty).   3
                                                  7,522   1   2
          Less: Audit Fee due - year to
                        31/12/1934.   8   8   0

Dec. 31   " Dividends on Investments viz:

          Bank of Ireland Stock to 30/6/36   113 11   0
          4½% Land Bonds to 31/12/36.   54 12   3
          5% Dublin Corpn.Stock to 31/12/36   69 15   0

          " Bank Interest on Credit Balance.

          " Refund of Income Tax.

          " Profit on sale of Investments:
            £950 4½% Land Bonds.

31st December, 1936.   CR.

PAYMENTS.

1936.
Dec. 31 By Grants to Lady Dudleys Nursing Home
                    Scheme.   375   0   0

        " Grants to Dependents.   222   0   0

        " Clerical Assistance.   160   5   0

        " Travelling Expenses.   22   1   0

        " Audit Fee for year to 31/12/1935   8   8   0

        " Printing, Typing & Stationery.   11   9   4

        " Postages etc.   2   12   1

        " Cheque Book.   16   8
                                                              802   12   1

        " Balance in favour of the Fund viz:

            Investments at cost:
                £1085.5.8 Bank of Ireland Stock   3,303   19   5
                £1316   4½% Land Bonds.   1,275   6   10
                £1800   5% Dublin Corpn.Stk.   1,710   0   0
                                                   6,289   6   3

            Cash in National Bank – as adjusted   813   16   4

            Cash on hand – petty.   9   5   7

            Income Tax Refund due.   133   8   2
                                                   7,245   16   4
            Less: Dividend due Purchaser of
                  £500 4½% Land Bonds.   8   14   5
                                                              7,237   1   11

                                                              8,039   14   0

November, 1927.

WEST COAST DISASTER NATIONAL
(RELIEF) FUND.

My dear

I have received your generous subscription to the National Fund for the immediate relief of the many dependents of the victims of the recent tragedy on the coasts of Galway and Mayo and to make such future provision for them as may be necessary.

I desire to express to you the very sincere thanks of the Committee and myself for your generous response to the National Appeal. It is a source of **great gratification to us to receive your donation so** promptly as it indicates that you have a real and practical sympathy for the stricken families on these wild and isolated seaboards.

Yours sincerely,

Liam T. Mac Cosgair

APPENDIX 3: *Letter of acknowledgement from the West Coast Disaster National Relief Fund Committee sent to those who donated money to the fund.*
APPENDIX 4: *(pages 109 and 110) Letters to Monsignor McAlpine and John Healy from the Land Commission in connection with the settlement of lands after the Cleggan Bay disaster.*
(Documents courtesy of the National Archives, Dublin)

P.S. 1418/27

24th November, 1927

Dear Canon McAlpine,

I am in receipt of your letter of the 16th instant, and have obtained from the Commissioners a report regarding the Lighton and other properties you mention. The Commissioners are fully alive to the acute congestion which exists in the Lighton Estate (Rossadelisk), and to the urgent necessity for the abolition of the rundale system there with as little delay as possible, and with this end in view they are negotiating for the acquisition of certain lands in the vicinity. When acquired these lands will enable small rundale holdings on the Lighton Estate to be striped and rearranged. Considerable progress has been made towards acquiring these lands, particulars of which are as follows:-

Estate of Charles B. Freyer. (now Major Dermot Freyer)

    Lands of Rossadelisk   67 acres
       do   Mooreen ... 46 "

"Twining" Estate.

    Lands of Cleggan (Mrs Julia Hobarton)
      do   do   (Mrs Blanch Bailey)
      do   do   (Mrs Charlotte Browne)

Estate of the Representatives of Richard Kearney.

    Lands of Shinnanagh   642 acres
       do   "Omey Island" comprising
    Cloon 80 acres and Sturrakeen 30 acres.

O'Neill Estate.

    Lands of Doon, Maw and Boolard, containing 978 acres.

I have requested the Commissioners to do everything possible to expedite the proceedings for the acquisition of these lands. You may rest assured that there will be no avoidable delay in the matter, and that the near future will see a beginning made towards the amelioration of the very unsatisfactory conditions prevailing in this area.

        I am, dear Canon McAlpine,

          Yours very sincerely,

Very Rev. P. Canon McAlpine P.P.,V.G.
   St. Joseph's,
    Clifden.

COPY/

Irish Land Commission,
Upper Merrion Street,
DUBLIN.
30th June 1928.

30835/28

A Chara,

With further reference to your letter of the 19th inst respecting the steps being taken by the Land Commission to relieve congestion in the Rossadillisk Area, Clifden, County Galway, I am directed by the Land Commission to state that possession has been obtained of the holding of Charles B. Freyer on the Lighton Estate and where the lands are not in the occupation of sub-tenants temporary lettings have been made pending final distribution.

With regard to the holdings of the Reps. of Richard Kearney, deceased, in the Townlands of Omey and Aughrusbeg on the Berridge Estate which are the subject of an Administration Suit, an Order has been made by the Court for the sale of the tenancy interest therein and the Land Commission is negotiating with the parties entitled with a view to arranging a price at which the lands may be acquired.

The Land Commission has fixed the price payable on the acquisition of the lands of Shinnanagh and a scheme for the distribution of these lands will be prepared as soon as possible.

The Land Commission is proceeding in the matter of the Estates of Dr. Sydney Brown and Mrs. Blanche Bailey but are not at present acquiring the Estate of Mrs. Julia Hobarton.

In the O'Neill Estate the price of the lands to be acquired of the lands has been fixed and a scheme for the distribution of the same will be prepared as soon as possible.

Mise, le meas mor,

JAMES T. DRENNAN.

John Healy Esq.,
Room 9, Government Bldgs.,
Merrion Street,
DUBLIN.

Telegrams : "Fisheries, Dublin."
Telephone : 61934

Ein-fhreagra ag an litir seo, is mar
seo ba chóir é stiúradh :—
(Any reply to this communication
should be addressed to : —)
    An Rúnaí
    (The Secretary)

fé'n uimhir seo : —
(and the following number quoted :—)

SAORSTÁT ÉIREANN

ROINN TAILTE AGUS IASCAIGH
(Department of Lands and Fisheries),

PLÁS CHILLDARA, 3
(3 Kildare Place),

BAILE ÁTHA CLIATH
(Dublin).

12adh Marta, 1931.

A Chara,

    I am directed by the Minister for Lands and Fisheries
to state in reply to your communication of 9th instant
on the subject of extending to the Rossadillisk area the
scheme of Gaeltacht Industries controlled by this Department
that an instructress in circular machine knitting of hosiery
is now at Cleggan and suitable premises have been obtained.
Ten knitting machines are installed in the premises, and
employment will be given to 12 workers from the Rossadillisk
and Claddaghduff districts. According as these girls become
fully proficient it is intended to issue machines to them for
working in their homes, thus leaving the centre free to take
on more learners.

                Mise, le meas,

John Healy, Esq.,
Secretary,
West Coast Disaster National (Relief) Fund,
Government Buildings,
DUBLIN.

APPENDIX 5: *Letter to John Healy from the Minister for Lands and Fisheries regarding the*
installation of knitting machines in the Rossadilisk and Claddaghduff districts.
(Documents courtesy of the National Archives, Dublin)

'Marie Feeney has put together a very readable and poignant account of a terrible event, which is etched in the memory of her own family and community.'

Connacht Tribune, December 21, 2001

'This is a well researched and comprehensive account of the tragedy that occurred on October 28th, 1928. The book is eminently readable, and the selection of photos from the period is excellent . . . of interest far beyond the immediate, . . . a testament to the hardships endured by the villagers in normal circumstances, exacerbated by the enormity of this tragedy. It deserves a place on every bookshelf.'

Eithne Hannigan

'Marie Feeney is to be congratulated on bringing together in one book all the facts, fiction and folklore surrounding the Cleggan and North Mayo disasters of that fateful night in October 1927.'

Cormac Ó Cionnaith, Mayo News, October 24th, 2001